The Three Angels' Good News

Sherrilee Fish

TEACH Services, Inc.
P U B L I S H I N G
www.TEACHServices.com • (800) 367-1844

The author assumes full responsibility for the accuracy of all facts and quotations as cited in this book. The opinions expressed in this book are the author's personal views and interpretations, and do not necessarily reflect those of the publisher.

This book is provided with the understanding that the publisher is not engaged in giving spiritual, legal, medical, or other professional advice. If authoritative advice is needed, the reader should seek the counsel of a competent professional.

Copyright © 2021 Sherrilee Fish
Copyright © 2021 TEACH Services, Inc.
ISBN-13: 978-1-4796-1389-2 (Paperback)
ISBN-13: 978-1-4796-1390-8 (ePub)
Library of Congress Control Number: 2021911013

Unless noted otherwise, Bible verses in this book are from the King James Version. Italics are from the original text, indicating words supplied by the translators.

Verses marked NKJV were taken from the New King James Version® (NKJV). Copyright © 1982 by Thomas Nelson. Used by permission. All rights reserved.

Published by

www.TEACHServices.com • (800) 367-1844

To my Junior Sabbath School class who came to church with inquiring minds and challenged me to study the topics well enough to be able to teach them.

To my three precious children: Gabriella, Lia Hope, and Beau. Your faith in my abilities is what encourages me to do and try. God knew exactly what He did when He gifted you to me and I can't wait for us to spend eternity together, with Him.

To my Father in heaven who challenged me to write a book for His glory, may His name be exalted as we share the message to the world, of the 3 Angels of Revelation 14.

Table of Contents

Introduction vii

Section 1   The First Angel 9
Chapter 1   Of Angels and Names 11
Chapter 2   What Fearing God and Giving Him Glory
            Looks Like 17
Chapter 3   "The Hour of His Judgment Is Come" 22
Chapter 4   Has the Hour of His Judgment Already
            Come?. 29
Chapter 5   Why Did the Great Disappointment Have to
            Happen?. 38

Section 2   The Second Angel 43
Chapter 6   Warning Lights. 45
Chapter 7   Who Do We Say the "Mother Church" Is?. 54

Section 3	**The Third Angel**	**63**
Chapter 8	Worship a What?	65
Chapter 9	The Beast and Its Image	69
Chapter 10	Patience of the Saints	77
Chapter 11	What Is It Worth to You?	81
Chapter 12	And Keep the Faith of Jesus	89

Introduction

And I saw another angel fly in the midst of heaven, having the everlasting gospel to preach unto them that dwell on the earth, and to every nation, and kindred, and tongue, and people, saying with a loud voice, Fear God, and give glory to him; for the hour of his judgment is come: and worship him that made heaven, and earth, and the sea, and the fountains of waters. And there followed another angel, saying, Babylon is fallen, is fallen, that great city, because she made all nations drink of the wine of the wrath of her fornication. And the third angel followed them, saying with a loud voice, If any man worship the beast and his image, and receive *his* mark in his forehead, or in his hand, the same shall drink of the wine of the wrath of God, which is poured out without mixture into the cup of his indignation; and he shall be tormented with fire and brimstone in the presence of the holy angels, and in the presence of the Lamb: And the smoke of their torment ascendeth up for ever and ever: and they have no rest day nor night, who worship the beast and his image, and whosoever receiveth the mark of his name. Here is the patience of the saints: here *are* they that keep the commandments of God, and the faith of Jesus. (Revelation 14:6–12)

These, my dear reader, are the three angels' messages of Revelation. Growing up as a Bible believing Christian, I knew they were important. I would hear the adults talk about them and, even at times, the preacher preach about them, but never did I really understand the conversations or sermons, and I most certainly was not able to tell my friends what they meant and why they were so important to our faith. I knew that Revelation was full of symbols and signs, but I did not know how to interpret them.

Recently, however, I have come to realize that the juniors I teach also don't understand or even know about the three angels' messages, and because of this reality, I believe God has put it on my heart to write a book that will allow even a young child to understand these important messages.

Here is an example of what one of my favourite authors, Mrs. Ellen G. White has to say about the three angels' messages: "Those who understand and receive them will be kept from being swept away by the many delusions of Satan" (*Early Writings*, p. 256). I don't know about you, but I certainly don't want to be tricked by Satan and his lies.

Additionally, Ellen White confidently declares: "The most solemn, sacred work ever given to mortals is the proclamation of the first, second, and third angels' messages to our world" (Letter 146, 1909). Wow! Sharing the three angels' messages with my junior class, my family, my friends, and anyone else is a very important job.

So then, let me start sharing with you right now, as we decode these messages together.

Section 1

The First Angel

Chapter 1

Of Angels and Names

> And I saw another angel fly in the midst of heaven, having the everlasting gospel to preach unto them that dwell on the earth, and to every nation, and kindred, and tongue, and people, saying with a loud voice, Fear God, and give glory to him; for the hour of his judgment is come: and worship him that made heaven, and earth, and the sea, and the fountains of waters.
>
> (Revelation 14:6, 7)

I am sure by now you might have heard sermons or seminars on Revelation, or even read some of the book for yourself? And if so, you would have quickly realized that it has a lot of symbolism. It talks about beasts, frogs, trumpets, and seals, just to name some of the symbols used in this very interesting book. All these symbols are not literal but figurative. Many people believe that, because Revelation is written with all these symbols, we should not read it. Many feel it might cause confusion and scare people to not want to read the Bible anymore.

The reality is, though, that Revelation is the only book in the Bible that promises a blessing to whoever reads it and keeps the truths found in it. "Blessed *is* he that readeth, and they that hear the words of this prophecy, and keep those things which are written therein: for the time *is* at hand" (Revelation 1:3). That should make us want to read, hear, and keep what Revelation is saying. I know I sure do, for it comes with a blessing if I do. Therefore, we will break up these verses in Revelation 14 and see what we can discover.

"And I saw another angel fly in the midst of heaven …"

If I were planning a visit to see my sister, who lives in the United Kingdom, I would start looking for plane tickets. I live in Australia, and the only other possible option to visit her would be to travel by boat, but that could take a couple of weeks. Going by plane would get me to her country in just over 24 hours. Then, with an additional four-hour drive, I can be at her front door. Flying is definitely quicker than walking, running, driving, or sailing.

We see in Revelation an angel who is flying in the sky, indicating that what he is doing is happening quickly. The angel being referred to here is a messenger or preacher—a person. We know this by looking at the original Greek word, *angelos*, which means "messenger." Thus, the "angel" in Revelation does not represent a literal angel from heaven that is flying through the sky, calling out with a loud voice. Rather, it is depicting communication that will be done by preaching and that will be done with great speed.

The angel, preacher, or messenger has an everlasting gospel message to share with all the dwellers of earth. Whatever language you speak, whatever skin colour you have, and whatever part of the world you live in, this message is for you, and it is for me!

What is the "everlasting gospel"? The "everlasting" part is easy; it means it will last forever. The "gospel" part literally means that it is the glad tidings or, you could say, the good news, about Jesus and His power to save us.

When He was telling His disciples about the signs of His second coming and the end of the world, Jesus said, "And this gospel [the good news of His saving power] of the kingdom shall be preached in all the world for a witness unto all nations; and then shall the end come" (Matthew 24:14). If we link Jesus' statement in Matthew to this first angel's message, which also refers to the gospel, we can conclude that the message of the first angel is a message that will spread just before the end of this world, when Jesus comes back a second time.

The angel, or messenger, is proclaiming with a loud voice, "Fear God, and give glory to him; for the hour of his judgment is come: and worship him that made heaven, and earth, and the sea, and the fountains of waters" (Revelation 14:7).

"Fear God ..."

This is the first part of the message. But how are we to "fear God"? Aren't we supposed to trust God and go to Him with all our cares, especially when we have sinned? Why would we be told to be scared of Him? Of course, that can't be. God does not want us to be scared or fearful of Him in a negative way. On the contrary, He says, "For I the LORD thy God will hold thy right hand, saying unto thee, Fear not; I will help thee" (Isaiah 41:13).

It has been suggested that there are between 136 and 146 "fear not" verses in the Bible, which tell us to no longer be scared. That is an impressive number of verses! Thus, when the verse says, "Fear God," it must mean something other than being scared of Him. The best place to find what is actually meant is to look at other verses in the Bible. A really neat exercise you can do on your own is to take a concordance or online search engine and look up all the verses in the Bible that have "fear God" in them. You will be surprised how many there are—literally hundreds. I am giving you only a few; you will need to look up the others.

- "The fear of the LORD *is* to hate evil: pride, and arrogancy, and the evil way, and the froward mouth do I hate" (Proverbs 8:13). *I am fearing God when I hate evil.*
- "Praise our God, all ye His servants, and ye that fear him, both small and great" (Revelation 19:5). *Fearing God will allow me to praise Him.*
- "Fear not: for God is come to prove you, and that his fear may be before your faces, that ye sin not" (Exodus 20:20). *The fear of God will help me to not sin and show where my loyalty lies.*
- "By faith Noah, being warned of God of things not seen as yet, moved with fear, prepared an ark to the saving of his house" (Hebrews 11:7). *The fear of God will lead us to obey Him, even when what He is asking does not make sense to us.*

The feeling of fear really has very little to do with the fear of God. Fearing God seems to be a decision involving obedience to Him, being totally committed to what He is asking of us, surrendering our lives to Him, and allowing Him to guide us in making choices in our lives.

"And give glory to Him ..."

Again, let us use the Bible to interpret the meaning and clarify the expression for us.

In Exodus, chapters 33 and 34, we find the story of Moses after the children of Israel had made and worshiped the golden calf. In the story, Moses moves the tabernacle outside the camp and goes into it to talk with God. Then, while Moses is in the sanctuary, he has a request for God. He asks to see God's glory.

God responds to Moses saying, "I will make all my goodness pass before thee, and I will proclaim the name of the LORD before thee" (Exodus 33:19). The next day, when Moses goes up the mountain to meet with God, God does pass by Moses, and He reveals His glory to Moses. We therefore conclude that God's glory, goodness, and name are synonyms with each other. They are one and the same thing.

Chapter 1: Of Angels and Names

When I found out I was going to have my first baby, getting all the preparation done was very exciting. There were so many things the baby was going to need—diapers, clothing, and a pram (baby carriage). My husband and I were going to have to make so many changes—like buying a new car that would fit the car seat.

However, the one task we took more seriously than any other was the task of choosing the right name for our baby. We were not overly worried about the sound or how the initials would look. Our biggest concern was the name's meaning. I did not want to call my child a name she could not live up to. Therefore, when we decided on the name "Gabriella," it was the meaning— "strong woman of God"— that caught our attention and caused us to choose it.

Names and people's characters have long been synonymous. Remember the story of Jacob and how he wrestled with God all night? He did not know it was God and thought it was someone trying to kill him. Jacob struggled all night and, eventually, just before daybreak, realized that he was wrestling with God. This is when Jacob then held on and would not let go until God blessed him. The blessing God gave him was a new name. "Jacob" means "cheater," and he no longer needed to be known as that. He had gained the victory over that sin, and now his name was changed to "Israel," which means "one who wrestled with God as a prince."

Saul, after his conversion, became known as Paul. Before his change of heart, Saul had been determined to wipe out all the Christians who were choosing to listen to and follow what Jesus' disciples were teaching as opposed to what the Jewish leaders were teaching. Saul was an angry and determined man, but after Jesus showed him the truth, he could not deny that he had been

> *Fearing God seems to be a decision involving obedience to Him, being totally committed to what He is asking of us, surrendering our lives to Him, and allowing Him to guide us in making choices in our lives.*

wrong. So, he then became known as "Paul," which means "little or small." I like to think it is because he realized that, in comparison to God, he really was just little and small.

We are told in Revelation that God will give us a new name when we get to heaven—one that will properly reflect our changed character. "I ... will give him a white stone, and in the stone a new name written, which no man knoweth saving he that receives *it*" (Revelation 2:17). Why do you suppose our names will be written on a white stone?

Well, in Bible times, if the king's court needed to decide whether a person on trial was guilty or not, they would use white or black pebbles to cast their vote. Black meant guilty; white meant not guilty. How exciting! God is going to give us new names to reflect our character. He casts His vote on our side, saying that we are not guilty because Jesus took our sins away.

Another interesting name change in the Bible is found in Daniel 1:7. It reads: "Unto whom the prince of the eunuchs gave names: for he gave unto Daniel *the name* of Belteshazzar; and to Hananiah, of Shadrach; and to Mishael, of Meshach; and to Azariah, of Abednego." These four Jewish boys had been taken captive, and now their heathen captor gave them names to give honour to the Babylonian heathen gods.

The boys' Hebrew names all gave glory to Jehovah God. "Daniel" means "God is my Judge." "Hananiah" means "God has favoured." "Mishael" means "who is what God is?" "Azariah" means "Jehovah has helped." From the record of Scripture, we can see that, although the heathen king gave them other names, they continued to give honour to the God of their fathers and did not allow their circumstances or surroundings to change their character.

When I allow my sinful character to be transformed into the beautiful character of Jesus, I am giving God glory.

Chapter 2

What Fearing God and Giving Him Glory Looks Like

Remember when we said that to fear God and give glory to Him was to do what His Word tells us to do and then to reflect His character in our own lives?

I do not know about you, but it always helps me to watch someone doing something and then to copy what they have done. I then understand what needs to be done to try to replicate it. I believe God knows that it is easier for us to copy others than to try to figure things out, and that is why the Bible is full of examples of the way people lived and the lessons they learned from their experiences. These examples can help us in our lives to avoid making the same mistakes or to copy their good examples to win in our war against sin.

Do you remember the story of Balaam? Balaam was a follower of God, but when the opportunity arises for him to make lots of money, he chooses the money instead of staying loyal to God. God then uses a stubborn, talking donkey to try to help Balaam see his error. When that does not help, God shows him an angel with a drawn sword, ready to kill. This deters Balaam, but, unfortunately, it does not turn him away from his wicked desires for money and wealth. That is certainly not an example I want to follow, how about you? You can read the whole story for yourself; it is found in Numbers 22–24.

Looking at bad examples can help, but looking at good examples is a way better option for getting the help we need. We know we can look at the example of Jesus' life here on earth with confidence. He lived a perfect, sinless life and gave us the perfect example to follow. He feared God and gave Him glory. In Jesus' own words, "I can of mine own self do nothing: as I hear, I judge: and my judgment is just; because I seek not mine own will, but the will of the Father which hath sent me" (John 5:30).

Jesus did nothing of His own accord; He heard and obeyed His Father's word; He feared God. Did Jesus reflect His Father's character? Most certainly! He said, "I and my Father are one" (John 10:30). Jesus' character was the same as His Father's. We can look at His example and know what God the Father is like. Words that come to mind are "kind," "loving," "patient," "caring," and "happy." Jesus and God the Father are all of these and more, and They would like us to be like Them. "Fear God and give glory to Him."

Daniel and his three friends are also very practical examples of what fearing God and giving glory to Him looks like. If you are a bit fuzzy on the details, go ahead and read Daniel 1; that will refresh your memory. We will just look at some of the highlights:

- These four young teenagers had been taken captive—away from their homes and families—to a land with strange ideas, practices, and religion.

Chapter 2: What Fearing God and Giving Him Glory Looks Like 19

- We are told that they were princes in their home country, but now they were made to serve a heathen king.
- They were clever and knowledgeable.
- They would need to take a stand in the king's palace, meaning they would need a strong character to stand up for what they believed.
- They knew their futures had been decided for them, as they no longer had a choice in their career paths.

Despite all of this, Daniel decided in his heart that he would not defile or ruin himself. He chose in his heart to fear God and give glory to Him. As a result of his choice, he could not possibly eat the unhealthy food that was being served at the king's table. Instead, he asked for a simple meal of pulse and water. Calling it "pulse" is another way of describing something that has been sown or planted. So, in reality, he was asking to eat fresh fruit, vegetables, nuts, seeds, and grains, and to drink only water.

The results after only ten days were incredible. (It is important to remember that he was recovering from starvation in coming back from the march from Judah to Babylon.) The four faithful boys were fairer and healthier than everyone else, and it was so obvious to see the difference that they never again needed to worry about having to ask for healthy options at the meal table. They were keeping God's word by being true to His requirements regarding looking after their bodies—His temple. Daniel and his three friends were blessed for it, and, as a result, they were able to reflect God's character.

Towards the end of the chapter, we learn that, among all the captives, there were found none like them. They were recognized as being ten times better in learning than all the educated and learned men in the kingdom. God blessed them because they were willing to fear Him and give Him glory.

Are there any habits in your life that could possibly be revisited and fine-tuned?

"Wait," I hear you say, "can what I eat and drink really be so important to my relationship with God?"

I will let the Bible answer that for you. "Whether therefore ye eat, or drink, or whatsoever ye do, do all to the glory of God" (1 Corinthians 10:31). Did you see that? It even uses the words "the glory of God."

Why do you suppose eating and drinking is so important? Could it be because, when you eat food that is different from what others eat, it will give you more opportunities to witness? Say, for instance, if you only have carrot and celery sticks in your lunch box at school, other children may ask you why, and then you can tell them that you are giving glory to God, eating healthy food. Hmm, it could work, but I suspect you would quickly grow tired of just carrots and celery, and then what could you eat? Think about it.

In the story of Daniel, he purposed in his heart not to defile himself. In connection with our previous verse in Corinthians, the truth is that Daniel, like Paul (the author of Corinthians), knew that what we eat and drink affects our minds and our ability to think.

Have you heard the saying, "Garbage in, garbage out"? Here it means that, if you are feeding yourself junk food every day, your body is going to produce junk results. There are many studies that have been done about the effects of food and drink on our bodies and minds, and the evidence is conclusive: you are, to a large degree, what you eat.

> *When we fear God, we allow Him to make changes in us so that we can glorify Him through our new characters and healthy habits.*

Therefore, if you have purposed in your heart not to defile yourself—and I really hope you have—then next time you are tempted to reach for the lollypop or chocolate bar, ask yourself the question, "Will this help me bring glory to God?" The answer should help you decide whether to proceed with that choice or seek an alternative, a healthy alternative. Initially it might be hard, but then all new habits are hard to start with.

God has provided so many healthy alternatives that will help you to practice good habits as you continually choose to give Him the glory. If you are unsure about what is good for your body, just remember what Daniel requested: pulse to eat and water to drink. Anything that has been planted is covered by the word "pulse," and it is easy for us to see that candy bars do not grow on trees, and then neither do packets of chips and boxes of biscuits (crackers).

Try to eat things that are as close to their original state as possible—an apple instead of an apple pie, a strawberry instead of strawberry-flavoured candy, and an orange or mango instead of orange or mango juice. What I am trying to say is that we should eat foods in their more natural state. Giving God the glory might seem hard in the beginning, but look at the benefits it had for Daniel and his three friends. I know that you too will be blessed abundantly by God because you are choosing to live and eat in a healthy way and giving Him the glory through it.

To summarise: When we fear God, we allow Him to make changes in us so that we can glorify Him through our new characters and healthy habits.

Chapter 3

"The Hour of His Judgment Is Come"

I have a brother who is three years older than I am. While we were growing up, he was the one who would take care of me while our parents were at work. Even while on school breaks, I was only permitted to go to the pool or the playground if my brother was going also.

Well, as it would happen, he was old enough to get his first motorbike. That did not mean I was old enough to get one, but it did mean that my brother was allowed to give me rides on his bike in our very spacious backyard, which had a rather steep embankment in the back corner. We would ride all around the yard and up an embankment, requiring more power and speed, and then we would go down the embankment and around the yard again.

Chapter 3: "The Hour of His Judgment Is Come" 23

Oh, this was great fun, and I don't remember exactly how long the thrill of it all lasted, but I do know that we gladly surrendered our pocket money and any spare change we could find to refill the fuel tank of that much-loved motorbike. As with most things in life, we children—and I in particular—quickly grew tired of only the backyard, and, because I had graduated from being driven around to driving by myself, we ventured onto the verge, or sidewalk, next to our house.

This experience provided instant gratification, and now we had a backyard *and* a verge on which to practice our driving skills. As you can imagine, before long, the gratification that came from riding on our verge had worn off, and we felt that the neighbour across the road from us had a much longer and better verge than ours. With caution, we looked both ways and safely pushed the bike across the road so that we could test for ourselves how much better the other side of the road really was.

We were careful not to ride it across the road, as that would have been illegal, for neither of us had a licence, and we were not allowed on public roads. We did not want to break any rules. However, as with so many things in life, the effort of getting off the motorbike to push it across the road was just too much, and soon we were confidently riding the motorbike from one side of the road to the other side, no longer feeling it necessary to get off and push, no longer feeling the need to obey the rule.

This all went well for a while, until a police officer appeared out of what seemed like nowhere. He kindly asked me for my name and age and then asked if my father was at home. He also did the polite thing and asked to see my licence. We both knew I did not have one yet. It was at this point that I realized I was in serious trouble. I did not have a license to drive the motorbike because I was four years too young.

Although my parents had warned us not to ride on the roads, we did not take it too seriously. Besides, we were just crossing the road and not literally driving on it, right? The officer asked us to push the motorbike home and said he would be back later to speak to our father because we had told him that Dad was at work.

I went home in fear. I feared the judgment that this law-enforcing officer was going to pronounce against me and that it would give me a criminal record that I would have against my name for the rest of my life. Would I ever be able to get a licence? Would I ever be able to drive? The rest of the day passed by very slowly indeed, and I could not wait for my dad to get home. I needed to know what my fate was going to be.

Later that afternoon, after my dad returned home from work and was busy outside, I saw the police car pull into our driveway. The moment of truth had arrived, and I did not know if I should go out and meet it or stay in my room and hide. I think I must have done a little of both. For what seemed like an eternity (though it was probably only a few minutes), I hid in my room, and then I decided to go out and hear what the adults were discussing.

The officer was talking to my father, explaining to him what we had been doing and how we had broken the law. My father listened, apologized on our behalf, and then promised that it would not happen again. I think he already saw on my face that I was more than prepared to keep that promise. And then it was all over. We had been judged by the law-enforcing officer; we were guilty of the crime; but most importantly, we had received grace. That grace was enough to keep me in the backyard for the rest of the motorbike's life.

> *I went home in fear. I feared the judgment that this law-enforcing officer was going to pronounce against me and that it would give me a criminal record that I would have against my name for the rest of my life.*

The first angel says, "Fear God, and give glory to him, for the hour of his judgment is come." We know from the previous chapter that he is not saying that we should be afraid of God but, rather, that we should do what God requires because judgment is about to take place. The thought of judgment does conjure up feelings of fear and torment because we all know we have sinned and deserve to be punished.

There is a beautiful text in the Bible that says, "All we like sheep have gone astray; we have turned everyone to his own way; and the LORD hath laid on him the iniquity of us all" (Isaiah 53:6). Yes, we have all sinned, but Jesus has taken that sin upon Himself and paid the death penalty so that you and I do not have to pay the penalty, which we never could do ourselves.

Then, if Jesus has taken the penalty of the sins I have committed, is there a need for a judgment? Are all sins not forgiven? Well, technically yes, all sins *can be* forgiven because Jesus took all the sins of the world upon Himself and has sufficient grace for everyone. The reality is, however, that He cannot forgive the sins that are not confessed to him and given up.

For instance, if I have a habit of lying and find it very convenient to use this habit to get myself out of trouble on a regular basis, Jesus cannot take that sin and forgive it because I am not giving it to Him; I am choosing to hold onto it. Because I am choosing to hold onto it, I am, in effect, choosing to take the punishment for that sin myself. God will never force you or me to do something we do not want to do, even if it is going to cause us damage and harm. God respects our choice too much to force us to do anything we do not want to do.

However, God does give us plenty of warning and the opportunities we need to see that what we are doing is going to lead us on a path of self-destruction. Most of all, He offers us more grace than we need. We find such grace promised in Romans 5:20: "But where sin abounded, grace did much more abound." It is God's amazing grace that will give us power to resist our sinful habits and overcome them so we can reflect His perfect image.

Examples of Investigative Judgment

How does all this tie in with our judgment, you may ask? To answer we need to look at how God judges. First, let us look at the story of Adam and Eve just after they had sinned. God had warned them about Satan and his lies; He had asked them to stay together; He had given them everything they could ever need or want, as far as food was concerned; and He gave them clear instructions regarding one particular tree. Every tree was available from which to eat except for the one tree from which God asked them to stay away.

However, in the story, Eve eats of the tree, then Adam chooses to eat from it after she convinces him that it is good. Knowing that they had sinned, because He knows everything, God chooses to go and meet with them as He always has done, but He does not find them at their usual meeting spot because they are hiding. God then performs an investigative judgment, asking several questions: "Where *art* thou?" (Genesis 3:9). "Who told thee that thou *wast* naked? Hast thou eaten of the tree, whereof I commanded thee that thou shouldest not eat?" (Genesis 3:11). "What *is* this *that* thou hast done?" (Genesis 3:13).

God asks questions about the day's events, not because He needs to be told but because He wants the universe and all those involved to know and understand that He is fair and just. If God put Adam and Eve out of the garden without giving the rest of the universe an opportunity to see, hear, and understand what happened, some angels might be tempted to think that God is not as fair as He claims to be. All through the Bible, we see stories of God's coming down to earth and first asking questions in investigation before passing judgment. See if you can find other examples.

In 1844, after much Bible study and prayer, a group of believers came to realize that Jesus is our High Priest in heaven and that He had, in 1844, entered the Most Holy Place in the heavenly sanctuary to conduct what we will refer to as the investigative judgment. Remember, God investigates before He pronounces judgment. The process of the judgment that they identified would cover all the people who have their names written in the Book of Life, from the creation of the world until the present.

The people who do not want Jesus' forgiveness or anything to do with God's grace have chosen to have their names removed from the Book of Life. The names of those who have given their lives to Jesus and have asked Him to forgive and save them remain in the Book of Life.

Each name is read, and then the accuser, the devil, claims that person as his follower because he or she has sinned. But then Jesus, our High Priest, steps in and claims the person as His own because He has paid the price for those sins. That person is judged and found innocent because the blood of the Lamb, Jesus, has cleansed him or her.

This is what is meant by "the hour of his judgment has come" (Rev. 14:6, NKJV). According to careful calculations and following the symbolism of the prophetic festivals, this process actually started in heaven on October 22, 1844. God the Father and Jesus are busy with this process even now. They started with the cases of all the dead people first, and those who are alive while this process is going on are judged on a day-to-day, moment-by-moment basis. Right now, Jesus is claiming us as His own when we have asked Him to forgive us for doing wrong.

The reality is that, if we are dead, we can no longer confess our sins, but while we are alive, we can confess and ask for strength to no longer continue in our sinful habits. It is not a case of your name getting called upon and, because you have been awfully bad that day, you are lost for eternity. Oh no, it is a daily judgement process for us who are alive. Jesus is so closely busy in our lives, though we sometimes don't even realize it.

Jesus looks at us every day and says, "Today, we will work on your character reflection a little more so that by the end of the day, you will be reflecting My image a little more." And if you fail or slip up, Jesus says, "My child, I love you. Let's try again. This time, take my hand, and I will give you the power to resist and say 'no' to temptations." Whether it is a bad temper, lying lips, envy, or whatever you might be struggling with, Jesus is wanting to give you victory over that sin.

This does not mean we can put off asking Jesus for this victory over sin for a few days until we are ready to give it up. And why not? It is because we do not know what the future holds, and because there will be a time when Jesus will step out of the Most Holy Place, put off His high priestly robe, change into His kingly robe, and come and fetch us. The investigative judgment will be over, and all people will receive their reward based on the choices they have made.

Please, my dear friend, don't leave any sins unconfessed or think that there isn't a way for you to overcome whatever bad habit it is that you might have cultivated. God is more powerful than any habit you have, and Jesus has paid the price for your sins so you do not need to be a slave to old habits and sins. Confess them, put your hand in Jesus' hand, and walk with Him every day, moment-by-moment, for the rest of your life. You can do this through Bible study, prayer, and sharing your experiences with others of what God has done for you, and you will have nothing to fear in the investigative judgment.

Chapter 4

Has the Hour of His Judgment Already Come?

When I was back at school, I had a history teacher who could make the past come alive—almost as if he had been there himself. I believe that he's the one who planted in my heart the love I have for history. Some people, of course, think that history is boring and only for the old people. I want to assure you that history is quite exciting, and we have much to learn from history, or else we will be repeating the mistakes of the past all over again.

The author Ellen White made the following statement: "We have nothing to fear for the future, except as we shall forget the way the Lord has led us, and His teaching in our past history"

(*Last Day Events*, p. 72). In other words, if we can remind ourselves of what has been done in the past, we can face what is going to happen in the future without fear.

William Miller was a farmer back in the 1800s who doubted that the Bible was inspired of God. He desperately wanted to know what truth was but was not convinced that he would find truth in the Bible. God had not given up on William, just like He does not give up on any of us, and, through a series of events, William started reading and then studying the Bible for himself.

The more he studied, the better he got to know Jesus, and soon he was convicted that he was a sinner who needed a Saviour. He realized that Jesus had paid the price for him and was offering him a gift of repentance and forgiveness. In Jesus, he found a friend.

With intense interest, William studied the books of Daniel and Revelation. He compared scripture with scripture and saw that the prophetic symbols of these books could be understood. He realized that history had happened exactly as it had been foretold by the visions and dreams of Daniel.

These truths further helped William realize that the Bible was inspired by God, and, before long, he came upon the vision in Daniel 8. What was particularly interesting to him were the words in verse 14: "Unto two thousand and three hundred days; then shall the sanctuary be cleansed." He had already realized through his studies that Jesus was coming back a second time to take His people home and then destroy sin forever. This verse in Daniel spoke about a time when the sanctuary would be cleansed, and it gave a time when this cleansing would happen.

William reasoned that, if the starting point of this time prophecy of 2,300 days could be determined, he could calculate the end of it and when the sanctuary would be cleansed. He then concluded that the sanctuary must be referring to the earth and that

Chapter 4: Has the Hour of His Judgment Already Come?

the cleansing must refer to Jesus getting rid of sin by coming to earth, destroying the wicked, and taking the saints to heaven. He studied this out for about two years, and, in 1818, he reached the solemn conviction that, in about 25 years, Jesus was going to come back to earth to redeem His people. Oh, this filled William with such joy! Jesus was coming, and it was going to happen really soon!

How do you feel when you have good news to tell someone? I know that, when I have something exciting to share, I can hardly wait to tell others so that they too can experience the joy and excitement that I am experiencing. This is what William felt. He wanted to share

He realized that history had happened exactly as it had been foretold by the visions and dreams of Daniel.

this wonderful news with everyone, but there was one thing holding him back. William was concerned that people would accept what he said without first searching it out for themselves. He was also anxious that he might have made errors in his calculations or possibly misunderstood something in the prophecy, so he hesitated to tell anyone what he had discovered because he did not want to mislead them. For another three years, he restudied his findings, coming at it from every possible angle to see if he had somewhere misapplied some concept, truth, or understanding.

This process just further convicted him of how right he was in his position that Jesus was indeed going to cleanse the sanctuary very soon. The conviction that he needed to share this with others now rang loudly in his ears. Every day, he would hear, "Go and tell the world," over and over in his head. Here and there he started telling a few people as the opportunity arose, all the while praying that a minister or preacher would feel called to proclaim this message to the world.

For nine years, he continued like this, hoping someone would take the message and run with it because he did not feel confident to do it himself. The voice in his ears grew louder and more intense, and, one morning, William made a deal with God. He hoped this would silence the voice. He agreed to "go and tell the world," but only if someone invited him to speak in public about the new truth of Jesus' soon return.

Comfortable that he had now done enough to silence the voice and confident that he would no longer be bothered by these thoughts, he got up off his knees. He had never been asked by anyone to speak in public regarding his findings, so he felt very safe in his bargain with God.

However, no sooner was William off his knees, someone was knocking at his front door. When he went to open it, it was his nephew, who had been sent by his father with an urgent request for Uncle William: "As the minister is away, Father would like for you to come and share your findings of Jesus' soon return with the congregation tomorrow," the young lad said.

William was upset and stormed past the boy standing in front of him. He was angry with God and walked to a grove of trees near his house. Here he wrestled with God for an hour, giving Him all the reasons why he should not be the one to give these messages. Finally, he submitted his will to God, and a peace and joy washed over him. If God wanted him to share, he would do it, for God would supply the courage and strength.

William lectured the following day, and his sermon was blessed by God to the extent that thirteen families, with the exception of two family members, were converted. A religious awakening followed. People realized that, if Jesus were coming soon, they needed to change the way they were living to be ready.

William was immediately urged to speak in other places, and, in nearly every place, it brought about a revival in the hearts of people to work for God. The good news of Jesus' soon return was spreading fast. Not everyone was excited about the news, and those who opposed the message teased and made fun of those who accepted the truth that Jesus would return in only a few short years.

William, however, was not the only one who was sharing this new truth at this time. In England and other parts of Europe, there were others who too had come to understand that Jesus would be returning soon. The news spread quickly, and the world was awakened to the reality that Jesus was going to be returning soon and

Chapter 4: Has the Hour of His Judgment Already Come?   33

that bad habits and ugly characters needed to be changed to be able to meet Him when He came.

There were a few dates set as to when they thought it might happen, but the date of October 22, 1844 was the date that had the best evidence and the most biblical backing. It was thought and believed that, on this day, the world would come to an end and that Jesus would fetch those who chose to believe in Him and follow His ways, and He would then cleanse the earth from all wickedness.

The day of October 22, 1844, came and went, and many people were very disappointed. In fact, the day is referred to as the "Great Disappointment" of 1844. Those who loved Jesus and longed to see Him return believed that the Bible was true and knew that, somehow, they had made an error in their interpretations—not in their interpretation of the time of the prophecy but in the meaning of "the cleansing of the sanctuary."

They prayerfully went back to God's Word, their only source of truth, and finally came to understand that the sanctuary, which they had thought was the earth, was in fact referring to the job or ministry that Jesus was now performing in heaven. Do you remember that God had given the children of Israel an incredibly special gift when they were still living in tents in the wilderness? He showed Moses a little glimpse of how things work in heaven and what His home, or sanctuary, looks like. God then asked Moses to make an exact, scaled-down version of the heavenly sanctuary so that everyone on earth could see and understand His plan of salvation for a lost and dying world.

The sanctuary was made up of three divisions, or compartments. The first was the outer court. Here they sacrificed an animal on the altar of sacrifice and washed their hands and feet in the laver. The sacrifice represented Jesus, who would give His life in place of ours so that we can live with Him forever. The lamb that was presented as the sin offering had to be without deformities and sickness, just as Jesus was Himself without sin.

The laver where the washing happened represented baptism. Jesus set the example with His own baptism. Sprinkling water on your head is not a baptism. You need to go under the water and

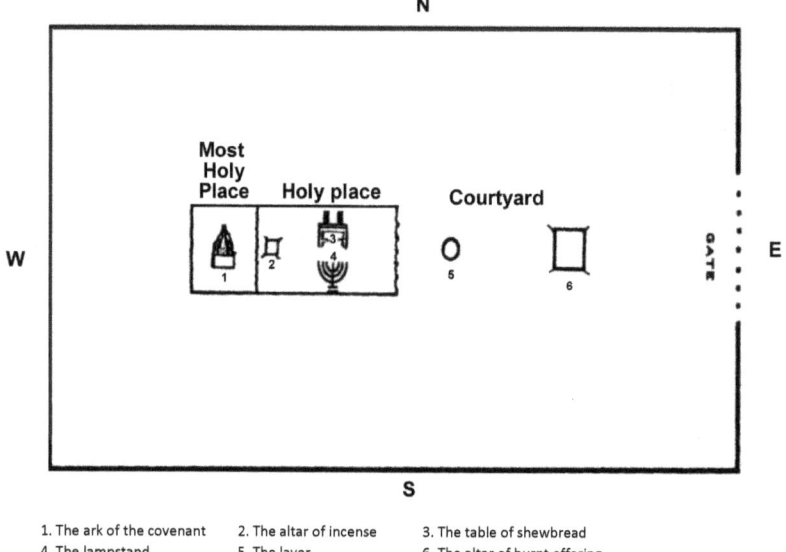

1. The ark of the covenant   2. The altar of incense   3. The table of shewbread
4. The lampstand   5. The laver   6. The altar of burnt offering

come up out of it to be baptised. This symbolizes dying to sin and being born again, or being resurrected, to a new life in Jesus.

The next division of the sanctuary was called the Holy Place. In this compartment were three items of furniture. First was the table of showbread, second was the seven-branched candlestick, and third was the altar of incense.

The table of showbread represents Jesus as the Bread of Life. As we need to eat food every day to stay alive, so also do we need to spend time with Jesus every day to stay spiritually healthy and alive. Just like we eat bread, and it becomes part of us, we need to make Jesus a part of us through studying His Word every day.

The seven-branched candlestick, which was the second piece of furniture, represents Jesus as the Light of the world, reminding us that we too need to shine our lights to the world in which we live. "How do we shine our lights," you might ask, "since we are not little fireflies?" Well, this world is dark because of sin, and, when we live our lives so others can see Jesus in us, we are shining our lights.

The third piece of furniture in this compartment was the altar of incense. Daily incense was burned on this altar, and the smell would rise to heaven. The smell was sweet and reminded everyone that their prayers were going up to God continually as a sweet-smelling incense before His throne. Jesus, who stands by God's throne, now takes our prayers and presents them to the Father because, on our own, we cannot come to God and talk to Him. His glory is so glorious that it would consume us. Through Jesus our High Priest, we can come to God the Father. Jesus takes our sins and then presents us to the Father as someone who has never committed any sins.

The third division, or compartment, of the sanctuary was called the Most Holy Place. The only item of furniture in it was the ark of the covenant. Inside the ark were the tables of stone upon which God wrote the Ten Commandments with His own finger. The ark of the covenant was a box covered in pure gold, and it had a lid on it. Two angels were on the lid, looking towards each other, with their wings stretched over the ark, touching each other. The lid of the ark was referred to as the mercy seat. It is here that God's presence was made visible in the form of a light called the *Shekinah glory*. The lid of the ark represented God's throne in heaven.

By now you get the picture that the sanctuary was not only a place for God to stay and make His presence known to the children of Israel, but it was also full of symbolism that depicted what Jesus was doing for us and the example we are to follow. There is still so much more for us to consider, but such details will have to wait for another discussion. It is sufficient to say that the sanctuary and its services are important because they reflect what has taken place, what does take place, and will take place in heaven.

All year round, the priests would sacrifice lambs as a representation of the sacrifice that the Lamb of God would make on behalf of us as sinners. The priest would take the blood from the slain lamb into the Holy Place and place it upon the horns of the altar of incense. Only once a year, on the Day of Atonement, the high priest would go into the Most Holy Place. This day was a most solemn and serious day, and everyone was expected to spend the day in fasting, prayer, and deep heart searching, while the high priest was inside the tabernacle making a sacrifice on behalf of all the children of Israel. The Day of Atonement was the very last service performed by the high priest during his yearly ministration.

As the Bible students of 1844 came to better understand the ceremonies and symbols, they realized that Jesus had, in fact, not come to cleanse the earthly sanctuary but had entered the Most Holy Place in heaven where He was offering His sacrifice of dying on the cross before the Father so that all who believe in Him should not perish but have everlasting life. Jesus is doing the last job as our High Priest before He comes to fetch us.

> **Jesus is doing the last job as our High Priest before He comes to fetch us.**

"What exactly is this job?" you may ask. The answer is that, just as the high priest in Old Testament times had to take the sins of the children of Israel on himself by taking the blood of the sacrificed lamb and sprinkling it on the mercy seat, symbolizing that the blood covered the people's sins, so Jesus too is standing before God's throne, the mercy seat in heaven, using His own blood that was shed on the cross to cover and forgive our sins.

All who have ever lived and asked God for forgiveness are presented to the Father. Jesus then steps between the Father and each repentant sinner and, showing His scars, reconciles the sinner to Himself. The sinner is forgiven, and his or her name remains written in the Book of Life. All people who believe in Jesus will have their name called in heaven's court.

Jesus has started from the beginning, right back to Adam, and is working His way through all the cases of those who have died. The people who are currently living He reconciles daily. Therefore, because we are still alive, every day our cases are brought before God's throne, and, as we confess our sins, Jesus steps in and forgives and cleanses us. That is the reason why we should go to Jesus as soon as we have done something wrong and been convicted by the Holy Spirit so we can ask Him to forgive us and strengthen us to not do that wrong again. He longs to give us His power to overcome our sinful habits.

Chapter 4: Has the Hour of His Judgment Already Come?

When this job of reconciliation (also called the investigative judgment) is completed, those who are still alive who believe in Jesus and the sacrifice He made for them will be living lives that reflect His character, and their names will be written in the Book of Life. Then and only then will Jesus take off His priestly robe, put on His kingly robe, and come and fetch us to go home with Him. How exciting, to think that we will be able to go and live with God for ever where there will never be any pain or sadness or worry or fear.

Chapter 5

Why Did the Great Disappointment Have to Happen?

Have you ever been so disappointed that you felt like giving up? Maybe someone made a promise to you and did not keep it so that it caused you to no longer trust that person. Maybe you had so looked forward to an event, like a birthday party, and you got all the food preparation done and decorated the area nicely, and then no one showed up. How disappointed you would feel! All the effort and no one bothered to come.

In 1844, as we mentioned in the previous chapter, students of the Bible experienced what is referred to as the "Great Disappointment." As we previously learned, William Miller and

Chapter 5: Why Did the Great Disappointment Have to Happen?

many others had been preaching that Jesus was to soon come back to earth to take His children with Him home to heaven. People got so excited that they sold their earthly possessions to print literature to share with others. Some closed theirs shops and businesses, as they wanted to devote all their time to spreading the good news of Jesus' soon return. Some people did not take this seriously at all and mocked and teased the Christians who were getting ready for Jesus to come.

On the anticipated day of October 22, 1844, many people went out to places in fields or on hills and waited for Jesus to fetch them. Others stayed in their homes. As the day wore on, it was becoming more and more evident that nothing was going to happen. They continued singing hymns, quoting Scripture, and encouraging each other, but still nothing happened. The day turned to night, and many of those gathered outside started heading home.

I can just imagine how sad, disappointed, and confused they must have been. Why did Jesus not come? What had they not understood? *Why? Why? Why?* The following day started just like all the others had before, and these advent believers had to face the fact that Jesus had not come as they had hoped and believed He would. They were called "Adventists" because they believed in the second advent, or second coming, of Jesus.

Some Adventists were so disappointed that they got angry and decided to not trust God or His Word any longer. They then joined the people who teased and mocked the Adventists. They felt so ashamed and embarrassed and their egos were so hurt that they no longer wanted anything to do with the Adventist belief and doctrine.

Others, however, knew that the Bible was true and that God does not make mistakes. They believed that the mistake was with them and their understanding, and so, with sincere prayer and Bible study, they started looking for the answer to their disappointment. Before long, God revealed to them in Scripture that the event that they had thought would be Jesus' second coming was, in fact, the beginning of His last job before He comes back to fetch us.

With that said, why did God allow these believers to experience such a disappointment? Could He not have revealed the truth to them sooner?

An Earlier Disappointment

Let me take you back to the time when Jesus was on earth. He has been teaching and preaching the gospel for almost three and a half years. He has raised people from the dead. He has made no secret about the fact that the purpose of His mission on this earth was to come to set the captives free from sin. He has preached it and lived it. Most all the religious leaders have rejected Jesus' teachings, and His own disciples are still arguing among themselves about who will have the best seat in His throne room.

The Sunday before Jesus is crucified, He asks two disciples to go and fetch Him the colt of a donkey that has never been ridden. If anyone asks why they are taking the animal, He tells them, they need to respond, "The Lord has need of it." The disciples straight away know what is happening based on current culture. Jesus is going to ride into Jerusalem atop the animal to proclaim Himself king.

They eagerly share this news with the friends of Jesus as they go to find the donkey. Just as Jesus has described it, they find the animal, and the news of Jesus' journey into Jerusalem spreads like wildfire. His entry is just like that of the Jewish custom whenever a king entered the royal city. Never has He allowed anyone to show Him such respect and honour, a fact that further convinces the disciples of their suspicions that Jesus is now ready to take the throne of David, rule over Israel, and defeat the Romans. The multitude of people that have gathered on this occasion can taste the sweet smell of victory over the Roman rulership and envision the Romans driven from their city, with Israel once more ruling themselves.

However, Jesus knows they are mistaken in their thinking. Why then does He allow them to think that He is going to establish His earthly kingdom? For over three years, Jesus has walked and talked with these people and told them that His kingdom is not of this world. No one has understood what He was meaning because they all had a vastly different expectation of their Messiah. They wanted freedom from the Roman Empire, but Jesus was offering them freedom from sin and sadness. He was offering eternal life, and they were looking for relief from temporal things.

Jesus has one week left before He is to be crucified. Entering Jerusalem this way has signed His death decree as the leaders of Israel will stop at nothing to get Him out of their way now. Jesus has become the focus and talk of everyone. People who have come to Jerusalem from all parts of the world to celebrate the Passover at the end of this crucial week are talking and watching His every move.

Jesus knows that by the end of this week, there will be a "great disappointment." He will be crucified and buried in a tomb. People will ask why, will be led to search the prophecies, and will find that Jesus' mission on earth was fulfilled exactly as the prophets have prophesied. The good news of Jesus the Messiah, who allowed the people to crucify Him, and His true kingdom will be taken to all the ends of the earth, and many converts will be won to the faith of His saving power. Here we can clearly see that Jesus allowed the misunderstanding, as its effects will accomplish a much greater good.

People will ask why, will be led to search the prophecies, and will find that Jesus' mission on earth was fulfilled exactly as the prophets have prophesied.

The Later Disappointment

A similar situation occurred in 1844. Because the believers did not understand the "cleansing" of the sanctuary in Daniel 8:14, they went out and preached that Jesus was soon to return to cleanse the earth. They were convinced that the sanctuary meant the earth. Many people became converted and realized that the lives they were living were selfish and evil, and a great revival started taking place all over the world.

People realized that they had neglected to read God's Word and follow His instructions. They were waking up from a sleep-like state of religion and making the many changes that were necessary. If the misunderstanding of the sanctuary did not occur, they would not have preached the Word of God with such urgency, and the revival that happened because of it would not have transpired. God was able to use the misunderstanding for everyone's greater good, just as He always does because "all things" do "work together for good to them that love" Him (Romans 8:28).

Section 2

The Second Angel

Chapter 6

Warning Lights

> And there followed another angel, saying, Babylon is fallen, is fallen, that great city, because she made all nations drink of the wine of the wrath of her fornication.
> (Revelation 14:8)

Another angel joins the scene. The first angel does not leave, for he continues with his mission of proclaiming the very nearness of Jesus' soon return and the importance of worshiping the God who created heaven and earth.

This second angel does not say much, but what he is saying is a warning. Why do we have warnings? Is it wise to ignore them?

Only recently, I am ashamed to say, have I been taking one warning in particular very seriously. I have been driving a car ever since I was legally able to do so. I could not wait! Two weeks after my eighteenth birthday, I was booked in and taking my driving test. (In the country I am from, you could only get your driver's license at age 18.) I was grateful, joyful, and excited when I passed the test.

I have been driving for many years, but recently the Holy Spirit has impressed upon my mind the fact that I have kind of ignored a warning sign. When approaching a traffic light, there are three possibilities for the next move. Little children learn a rhyme to help them remember it. In fact, it so important to obey this system that children learn the meaning of the warnings many years before they even learn to drive. The rhyme goes like this:

> Stop, says the red light;
> Go, says the green light;
> Wait, says the amber light twinkling in between.
> We all shall obey them, even the queen.

You know this warning system, right? We stop on the red light and proceed on the green light. However, I think there is some confusion regarding the yellow light that sits in the middle. I used to be one of those confused individuals. I treated the amber light warning to mean "press down a little harder onto the gas pedal to make sure you get through the intersection and not have to sit at the red light."

However, I have been clearly convicted since that it is a warning light, not a get-through-quick light. I am expected to approach a set of lights with caution; if it turns amber, I have already begun to slow down and am ready and able to stop as the red light is about to shine. Well, this has been a most interesting concept to my brain as I have been so used to ignoring the warning.

Thankfully, I have three faithful little witnesses with me in the car most of the time, and they comfortably warn me or even gently rebuke me when I forget to heed the amber light warning. Best of all, I have a patient Father who is constantly reminding me, and I can say that I now treat the amber light warning with respect. Warnings are not bad; they are there to keep us safe from danger.

"Babylon is fallen, is fallen."

The second angel is warning us. It is like the amber light of the three angels' messages in Revelation 14. As with many of Revelation's word pictures, code words are being used. To understand what a verse is saying, we need to understand the code. What better place to decipher the code than in the Bible itself? Okay, so our verse begins with "Babylon is fallen, is fallen." What do we know about Babylon?

Remember, a few chapters back, we spoke about four special young people, Daniel and his three friends, and how they were taken captive by the Babylonian king. We know they lived in Babylon, but during Daniel's lifetime, Babylon was attacked and overthrown by the next ruling power, which was the Medes and Persians.

> *The second angel is warning us. It is like the amber light of the three angels' messages in Revelation 14.*

Could the angel be warning us about the time that Babylon was invaded and conquered by Medo-Persia? I don't think so; rather, I think it is telling us what the author of Revelation possibly wants us to remember about what happened the night Babylon was overthrown. It was the ruling empire of the then-known world, and, in one fateful night, it was overthrown without much effort by the Medo-Persian army. We can read about it in Daniel 5.

Belshazzar was king in Babylon and the grandson of king Nebuchadnezzar. He was reigning because his father did not want the responsibility of ruling a kingdom. Belshazzar was very much aware of his grandfather's incredible story of conversion and knew about Daniel and the God whom he served.

We find Belshazzar in the middle of a great feast that he is hosting for 1,000 of his lords. There is not much detail in the Bible about the feast except that they were all drinking wine and, at this point in the story, very drunk. The Bible warns us: "Wine *is* a mocker; strong drink *is* raging: and whosoever is deceived thereby is not wise" (Proverbs 20:1).

Alcohol, in any form, is not a drink that we should even consider putting into our bodies. The awful effects of alcohol consumption in our world are visible everywhere. It removes from people the ability to reason with a sound mind so they make decisions and choices that cause heartache and sadness. If I can give you one bit of advice, do not even be tempted to try it—not even once. Proverbs is full of warning verses as to why we should never try alcohol.

So, we know that Belshazzar had been drinking and that his ability to make good choices and decisions has been lost. In his state of drunkenness, he orders his servants to bring to him the gold and silver vessels that his grandfather had taken from the sanctuary temple in Jerusalem. He wants to drink from these vessels.

How foolish! All the vessels from the temple in Jerusalem were dedicated to God, the Creator of heaven and earth. Belshazzar is clearly showing his disregard and lack of reverence for God by these actions. Although he has witnessed God's power in the lives of those around him, he chooses to praise the false gods of gold, silver, brass, iron, wood, and stone.

Belshazzar has taken that which is holy and made it common. In a sense, he has taken God's earthly sanctuary, with its symbolism, and disregarded its sanctity, using its vessels for his own pleasure when they were intended to be used for service to God.

That same night, Belshazzar sees a mysterious hand, writing a message on the wall of his banquet hall. He is so frightened by this phenomenon and message that he does not notice that his knees are knocking together or that the blood has drained from his face. The laughing and foolishness of a few minutes before are gone, and the king is no longer able to enjoy himself.

The queen mother is the one who reminds Belshazzar that Daniel knows the living God. Daniel is brought before the king and gives him the interpretation of the writing on the wall. King Belshazzar and the subjects of his kingdom have refused to humble themselves and give their hearts to the only true God. Therefore, God can no longer restrain the impending evil. That same night, Babylon is invaded, and Belshazzar is killed by the

Chapter 6: Warning Lights

Medo-Persian army under the rulership of king Darius. *Babylon has fallen*.

Getting back to the second angel's message, we ask: Is the point of the message to just get the reader to remember this bit of history, or is there more to it? We know that Revelation uses symbols and signs. Keeping the historic story in mind, let's find the meaning of the symbols and see if they make up a picture.

The name "Babylon" is derived from the word "Babel." ("Babel" is "Babylon" in the early Greek translation of Genesis.) In the Bible story of Babel, we remember how the people wanted to build for themselves a tower that would reach to heaven. This they believed would save them from any future destruction that God might want to visit upon them. Instead of making the Creator God their safety, they looked to themselves. How foolish! God had promised Noah that He would never again destroy the whole earth by a global flood, and He gave the rainbow as His sign of guarantee. The people building the tower clearly did not believe His word and were determined to oversee their own health and safety. In God's mercy and wisdom, He realized the terrible things that would result from everyone staying in one place, as opposed to spreading across the globe as He had asked them to do.

God chose to confuse their language. Neighbour no longer understood neighbour, and there was confusion as people could not communicate one with the other. In Revelation, we see that Babylon equals Babel, which equals confusion. Babel is therefore synonymous with confusion. The result? Those who could understand each other got together and moved to a place where they could live and start a new life, free from language barriers.

Babylon on a Beast

Revelation 17 talks about Babylon as a woman riding on a beast. A woman is symbolic of a church in biblical terms. When Jesus returns, He will come to fetch His bride—His church. A virtuous woman depicts a pure church following the doctrines of biblical truth. A vile woman represents a church that believes anything else and does not have the pure doctrine of truth. It is a church that is confused by false doctrines and traditions.

Tell me, do you need a lot of error for truth to become false? Say I gave you a whole glass of water to drink. Would you drink it if you were thirsty? What if I told you I just put one drop of poison in the water? Would you still drink it? "No!" I can hear you saying. Why not? It is a full glass of fresh water with only one tiny drop of poison in it. The truth of the matter is that just one drop of poison in a whole glass of water makes the water poisonous. That single drop has contaminated the water and potentially made it lethal to drink.

Just so it is with truth. You can have a whole system of religion full of biblical truth, but if there is a single grave point of error, the whole is contaminated and potentially lethal. Our enemy, the devil, does not really care what we believe, just so long as we do not believe the truth. He is subtly working to put just that one drop of poison into our truth to contaminate the whole.

Babylon represents a church that is false. There might be a whole lot of truth in her doctrines, but there are also doctrines that are false, poisonous, and lethal.

It's history lesson time. Remember a few chapters back when we spoke about 1844 and the Great Disappointment? Remember how there was a great revival, and everyone was sitting up, listening, and spiritually waking up from a sleep, realizing that changes needed to be made in their lives? Some people did it out of fear; some did it because others were making the changes; and some were sincere and desired to know the truth so that they could do God's will.

Before too long, the Bible students began to realize that what they had grown up believing was not necessarily biblical; they were traditions and habits that had been followed year after year, generation after generation. Protestants had come out of a church against which they had protested because they did not agree with the church's manmade doctrines, hence their name—*Protestants*. Unbeknown to them, there were still some beliefs they held that were not biblical.

One of those beliefs was that of worshipping on Sunday, the first day of the week, instead of Saturday, the seventh day of the week, which God blessed and sanctified from the beginning of world and also has instructed His people about in His Word. This was hard to come to terms with for many of the believers. For people to realize that they and their family had been doing something in error, when they were doing it sincerely, was a shock, and most people's first reaction—as it is today—was to kick against it and reject the new truth.

The other side of the coin was that, given that most Christians were keeping the first day holy, surely this should give it credibility, right? The reality, however, is that just because most people are doing something does not mean it is right. In most cases, it is actually a warning that there is error.

Look at the example of Noah. The majority chose not to obey the warning he preached and enter the ark. Noah and his family were a total of eight people and the only ones who lived to tell the tale of the flood. I have often warned my children: "If most people are doing what you are wanting to do, you can almost be sure it's not going to be safe to pursue it."

This was the case of these strange new truths emerging due to the diligent and sincere Bible study in which believers engaged after the Great Disappointment of 1844—truths around the sanctuary service and what the cleansing of the sanctuary really means, truths about what really happens to a person when they die, and the truth about the way we worship God and what day is really His holy day. For many years, people had believed and followed a doctrine that was not biblical, but now truth was shining on them like big floodlights that shine their beams on a playing field after the sun has gone down.

Some chose to accept the truth as found in the Bible. They realized that they had been doing things in ignorance, and, as Acts 17:30 tells us, "The times of this ignorance God winked at." There were many, though, and sadly the majority, who chose to continue doing things as they had been doing them for years and years. They chose the traditions of humanity over the clear "Thus saith the Lord" in His Word.

Do you know where the Protestant reformers had come from—what system of belief they had left to become Protestant believers? During the Reformation, they broke away from the Roman Catholic system of beliefs and began calling themselves "Protestants" because they were protesting the false teachings of the "Mother Church," as she was called. Unfortunately, it was the "Mother Church" that taught and enforced the tradition of Sunday observance as a sacred day.

In fact, the "Mother Church" claims that they have the power and authority to change God's law, and that is the reason they chose to change His day of worship to their own day of choice. In the next chapter, we will look at this more closely. It is also the "Mother Church" that teaches the concept of an eternally burning hell, where sinners supposedly burn forever, and many other concepts that are just not found in the Bible.

When the Protestants chose to continue with the traditions of the "Mother Church," they chose to show that they were actually accepting her authority over them as opposed to God's authority through the Bible. They surely had a lot of truth, but they chose to hold onto a little error, and, as with a drop of poison in a glass of water, we know that a little error is dangerous—even in a big cup of truth!

After the "Great Disappointment," a church denomination started growing out of a group of people who were only interested in what God's Word taught, not the traditions taught by the church. They did not set out to start a new denomination. Initially, they tried showing their home churches the errors they were finding, but eventually they were either asked to leave their church denominations or they chose to leave due to the rest of the church's unwillingness to see truth over error.

The messengers had already been proclaiming the first angel's message in the teachings of William Miller who taught about Jesus' work of judgment, but now they understood the warning of the second angel about the fall of Babylon and began to proclaim it. Did they proclaim this message because they did not like the other churches that continued worshiping on the first day of the week? No. The amber light does not turn amber because it sees a car approaching that it does not like. It turns amber because that is its job. We are all to warn people about false teachings and traditions because we don't want them to drink the glass of water with the drop of poison in it that could kill them.

It's also interesting to note, in studying these false teachings, that people accept them largely because they have not taken what God says as words of life and truth. They would rather keep the traditions of humanity as sacred while disregarding God's teachings in the Bible—much like King Belshazzar, who took that which was holy and dedicated to God and made it a common thing by using it to drink wine at his final feast.

> *The amber light does not turn amber because it sees a car approaching that it does not like. It turns amber because that is its job.*

God is holy, and what He has made holy, we should respect and keep holy too. I'm especially reminded of Exodus 20:8–10: "Remember the sabbath day, to keep it holy. Six days shalt thou labour, and do all thy work: But the seventh day *is* the sabbath of the LORD thy God: in it thou shalt not do any work." God is reminding us to keep holy what He has made holy. By refusing to keep the seventh day holy, we are going against what He has clearly instructed.

Many churchgoers know that they are worshipping on the wrong day, but, because it is convenient, they don't want to change. Either their families or most other Christians have been doing it for so many years that they don't want to do otherwise and be different. There are also many sincere, Bible-believing Christians who don't know that, by worshipping on any other day besides the seventh day of the week, they are following manmade laws and traditions. These people need to hear the warning of the second angel: Babylon is fallen, is fallen!

Chapter 7

Who Do We Say the "Mother Church" Is?

Have you ever been misunderstood by someone? Have you ever been forced to wear a label that did not apply to you and that really wasn't who you are?

When Jesus came to this earth as a baby, He had one mission: to show us what His Father is like and save us from our sinful selves. However, as He started His ministry, He was misunderstood by most of the people. Even His mother and close companions, the disciples, did not understand why He did things the way He did. They all misunderstood Jesus, and it was only after His death and resurrection that they came to understand the true nature of Jesus' mission.

Chapter 7: Who Do We Say the "Mother Church" Is?

Misunderstandings can cause a lot of hurt and sadness; they can also be scary and dangerous. For instance, if you misunderstand the label on a medicine bottle, you can be taking the medicine in the wrong way or in the wrong amount for your age and weight. That medicine can become harmful rather than helpful, as it was intended to be.

In Revelation, the name "Babylon" is given to a woman dressed in scarlet and riding on a beast with her name on her forehead.

> So he carried me away in the spirit into the wilderness: and I saw a woman sit upon a scarlet coloured beast, full of names of blasphemy, having seven heads and ten horns. And the woman was arrayed in purple and scarlet colour, and decked with gold and precious stones and pearls, having a golden cup in her hand full of abominations and filthiness of her fornication: And upon her forehead was a name written, MYSTERY, BABYLON THE GREAT, THE MOTHER OF HARLOTS AND ABOMINATIONS OF THE EARTH.
> (Revelation 17:3–5)

Understanding who this woman is will help us understand the warnings about her; misunderstanding who she is could cause us to be deceived and leave us feeling discouraged. Because it is a symbol used in the Bible, we are going to use the Bible to interpret what it means. Grab your Bible, if you will, and let's see what we can find.

First, turn to Revelation 17. There we find a clear description of the woman who rides on a beast. It is also important to note that verse 5 identifies her occupation and tells us what her name is. A woman in Bible symbolism represents a church. One of my children, a little while ago, asked me why Jesus never got married while He was here on earth. Well, Jesus has promised to be the husband to all who are His followers and believers (see Hosea 2:19). Marrying only one person would be unfair to everyone else, and we know that Jesus loves all of His children equally.

That does not mean that, if you are a male, you need to become a bride. No, it means that Jesus is using the symbolism of a bridegroom and bride to explain that He is intricately connected—as close as the connection between a husband and wife—to His faithful people. Jesus is married to His people by a promise to be their God, and His people have promised to be His alone.

In the Old Testament, the children of Israel were the faithful people. They were a group of people that God set aside as different from the other nations around them. They were a religious group, or church, and were meant to teach the other nations all about God and His love for them. Therefore, this woman on the beast also represents a church or religious group of people.

A few chapters back, we looked at the importance of names in the Bible, for they give us a description of someone's character. In Revelation 22:4, we are told that the redeemed shall see God's face, and His name shall be in their foreheads. We are pretty sure that everyone in heaven is not going to have to get a tattoo on their forehead. What the symbol of having God's name in the forehead means is that everyone will have a character like God's—they will think like Him and be good, kind, filled with His love, patient, joyful, and merciful, which are all wonderful attributes that describe God.

This woman riding on the beast also has her name on her forehead. She is called "Mystery, Babylon the great, the mother of harlots and abominations of the earth." Her name starts with "Mystery." She is known for her secretiveness and doing things in disguise. That is quite the opposite of God and His character. "Surely the Lord GOD does nothing, unless He reveals His secret to His servants the prophets" (Amos 3:7, NKJV). He does not do anything about which we have not been told or warned. God does not hide important things from us.

The word "Babylon" comes from "babel," which means "confusion." Do you remember the story in Genesis where the people wanted to make sure that they never got washed away by a flood? Even though God had made the promise through the token of the rainbow, they were determined to do things their way and to rely on themselves for salvation. As a result, He confused their languages so that they could not carry on with their silly plans, and the tower was called "Babel."

Chapter 7: Who Do We Say the "Mother Church" Is?

A harlot is a woman who does not stay faithful to her husband but, instead, she has an affair with someone else that is not her spouse. Again, that is not the kind of reputation on which you would build a trusting relationship. This symbolism denotes a church that does not stay faithful to God and His principles. She incorporates her own ideas and styles into her worship and does not stay true to the Word of God. "Ye adulterers and adulteresses, know ye not that the friendship of the world is enmity with God? whosoever therefore will be a friend of the world is the enemy of God" (James 4:4).

Being friends with the world means enjoying and practicing the things that this world offers. In Revelation 17:2, we are told that the kings of the earth have committed adultery with this false church, and the people of earth have been made drunk with the wine of her adultery. This sounds very much like what happened to King Belshazzar from Babylon, doesn't it? He took what God had made sacred—the temple vessels—and used them in a common way, showing no regard for God and His sacred services.

> *There is one church system that fits all these descriptions all too well, and my mom used to say, "If the shoe fits, wear it."*

This woman-church has caused the kings and people of the earth to be drunk or confused about what is right and wrong, about what is friendship with God and what is friendship with the world. There is one church system that fits all these descriptions all too well, and my mom used to say, "If the shoe fits, wear it." In other words, if someone says something about you, good or bad, and it is true, then you should wear the accusation. However, if it is not true, then don't let it bother you or let others try to put a "shoe" on you that does not fit.

The Roman Catholic system of beliefs has surely caused a lot of confusion (or "drunkenness") regarding the principles of God. Think back to when Martin Luther, a Catholic monk, discovered that we are saved by grace through faith as opposed to what he had been taught as a priest in his beloved church. He was taught that the way to forgiveness and salvation was through penance, a practice that often required physically hurting one's self as punishment or paying money to receive the forgiveness that one had requested.

The Roman Catholic Church has also happily and openly acknowledged that they have been responsible for changing the day of worship from Saturday to Sunday. They claim to have had the authority or right to do so. They also claim the authority to forgive sins and encourage their members to confess their sins to the priests. This is confusion and drunkenness over the principles of God.

That does not mean that all Roman Catholic believers are evil. Oh no—there are many sincere members who do not know the history and background and are ignorant of the truth. That is why the second angel is flying with a warning to all who are in Babylon so that they may realize that she is fallen, corrupt, and not standing on God's truth.

You are welcome to do your own research on the topic. A good place to start would be sabbathtruths.com, but I would just like to quickly share one quote with you that was published by the Roman Catholic Church:

> Sunday is founded not on scripture, but on tradition, and is distinctly a Catholic institution. As there is no scripture for the transfer of the day of rest from the last to the first day of the week, Protestants ought to keep their Sabbath on Saturday, and thus leave Catholics in full possession of Sunday.
>
> (*Catholic Record*, Indianapolis, Sept. 17, 1891)

There are also other similarities that the Catholic church shares with Babylon. For instance, she is dressed in purple and scarlet and decked with gold, precious stones, and pearls. When God asked Moses to make Aaron's high priestly robe, He specified the colours He wanted them to use. There is no coincidence that God wanted the colours to be, gold, blue, scarlet, and purple, with a breastplate of precious stones. Look it up in Exodus 28:3–5.

Chapter 7: Who Do We Say the "Mother Church" Is?

"But wait," I hear you say, "the woman in Revelation is not wearing blue." Yes, sadly not. Blue, in the Bible, represents a specific element, as do purple and scarlet. Purple would indicate royalty; scarlet would be representative of the sacrificial blood of Jesus; and blue represents God's law or commandments.

> And the LORD spake unto Moses, saying, Speak unto the children of Israel, and bid them that they make them fringes in the borders of their garments throughout their generations, and that they put upon the fringe of the borders a ribband of blue: And it shall be unto you for a fringe, that ye may look upon it, and remember all the commandments of the LORD, and do them; and that ye seek not after your own heart and your own eyes, after which ye use to go a whoring: That ye may remember, and do all my commandments, and be holy unto your God. I *am* the LORD your God, which brought you out of the land of Egypt, to be your God: I *am* the LORD your God.
> (Numbers 15:37–41)

It is interesting that God says in this passage that, if they remember His commandments, they will not go whoring after their own hearts. The Babylonian woman is called "the mother of harlots," so she has clearly forgotten God's commandments. If you google "Roman Catholic dress," the results of your query will reveal many images, and they all have red, purple, gold, and white, but blue is visibly missing. The colour that represents God's law is missing. This seems to be more than just a coincidence!

In Revelation 17:6, it states that this woman is drunk with the blood of the saints. Looking at the Dark Ages, when the Bible was taken away from the people and chained to the pulpits of the churches, makes me appreciate the fact that I have a Bible of my own and can read it whenever and wherever I want.

Psalm 119:105 tells us that God's word is a lamp and light. The Dark Ages were dark because God's Word was not readily available and many people had no idea what God said about important issues, so they were left to believe superstitious lies.

Martin Luther was impressed to read one of those chained up Bibles, and he discovered that the ideas and beliefs about salvation that he had been taught and that he was teaching were not according to the Bible at all. When he started asking questions, he was met with serious opposition and eventually had to hide for fear of being killed. This was the beginning of the Protestant Reformation.

As the Bible became available to the people and they could read it, light began to break upon them. The Reformation was met with severe opposition, and many people lost their lives for choosing to stand up for their new-found beliefs and no longer wishing to conform to the Roman Catholic Church's dictates. During the Reformation, the Roman Catholic Church was responsible for many, many deaths as they tried to stop people from learning the truths found in the Bible—truths about salvation, the forgiveness of sins, and many other truths that contradicted Rome's traditions and false doctrines. This woman-church surely has been drunk with the blood of the saints and those martyred for Jesus.

This similarity between the woman described in Revelation and the Roman Catholic Church is yet another identifying characteristic of the identity of the woman riding the beast. The Bible gives different descriptions of this church power, represented as a woman, but it always points back to the same institution. In the visions of Daniel 7 and 8, this institution is referred to as a little horn that has the eyes and mouth of a man, speaking blasphemous words and attempting to change times and laws.

The only law in God's Ten Commandments that refers to time is the fourth commandment, in which He calls His people to remember the Sabbath day to keep it holy. It is also, coincidently, the law that the Roman Catholic Church proudly claims that they had authority to change. This is yet another similarity that points us to the identity of the woman-church.

It is comforting to see how God has given us a warning in the second angel's message as well as clear indicators of who is being discussed. The truth is that when the books of Daniel and Revelation were being written, there was no Roman Catholic Church in existence, so God, in His wisdom, gave clues that would help us today. Following traditions or manmade laws regarding the worship of our Creator is dangerous, for it is going to lead us away from worshipping God as He has required and instructed us to do.

There are many churches today that are still following manmade traditions and laws above God's instructions and laws as found in His Word. A very clear and definite indication, if you are wondering, will be the day they keep holy and on which they worship. If it is anything but the seventh day of the week, in other words, Saturday, you can be sure they are following traditions and are in error.

It could be that they are ignorant about their error or not willing to admit it. Regardless of the reason, our warning is clear: Babylon is fallen, is fallen—fallen away from truth. Don't drink of her wine of false teachings, for it will cause you to fall too.

Section 3

The Third Angel

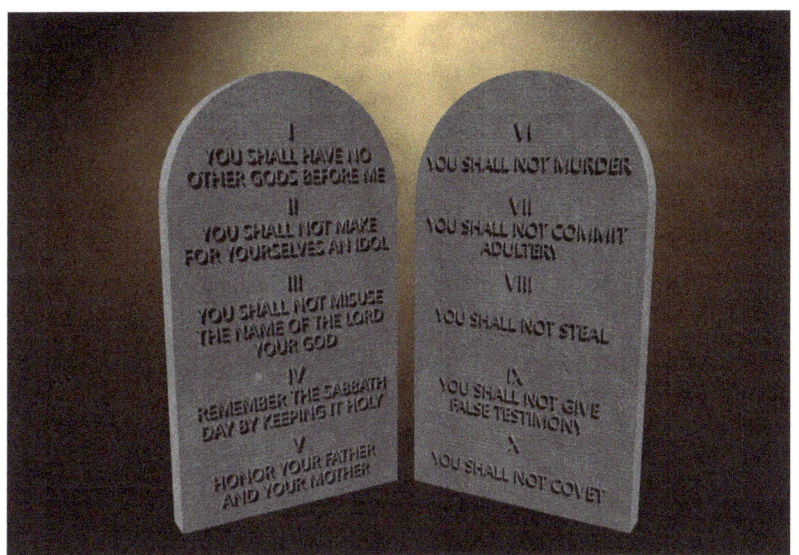

Chapter 8

Worship a What?

And the third angel followed them, saying with a loud voice, if any man worship the beast and his image, and receive *his* mark in his forehead, or in his hand, the same shall drink of the wine of the wrath of God, which is poured out without mixture into the cup of his indignation; and he shall be tormented with fire and brimstone in the presence of the holy angels, and in the presence of the Lamb: And the smoke of their torment ascendeth up for ever and ever: and they have no rest day nor night, who worship the beast and his image, and whosoever receiveth the mark of his name.

(Revelation 14:9–11)

In India, the rat is regarded as sacred. There is a temple where rats are protected, and people go to worship and take offerings of food for these little creatures. The reason for this is that the locals believe a goddess died and has returned to live here on earth again in the form of a rat. It is also believed that, if you eat of the food on which one of these rats has nibbled, you have received high honour.

While black and brown rats are everywhere, people believe that, if you spot a white rat, good luck is coming your way because you have been blessed by the goddess that is living in these rats. Indian people travel from all over the nation to pay tribute and give worship and homage to these rats, and tourists from all over the world travel to see this temple. Some estimate there are about 20,000 rats living in and around this temple.

I am reminded of a very interesting spectacle that happened way back in Bible times. You will find the story in 1 Kings 12:25–33. I'll give you a little background first. Solomon was made king after his father David died. Solomon built the temple; it took him seven years to complete it. Then he went on to build a palace for himself, which took thirteen years to build.

Solomon married many wives during his reign as king, and, to support his lavish lifestyle and care for all his household, he demanded great taxes from the children of Israel. This made them angry towards their king. In Solomon's old age, a prophet declares that God is going to divide the kingdom into two. Ten tribes will go and make Jeroboam their king, but, for David's sake, two tribes will remain under the rulership of David's family.

Solomon dies, and just as God has said, the kingdom divides. Solomon's son, Rehoboam, takes the throne, and as king, he foolishly listens to his friends instead of the wise counsel of the older men. He taxes his people even more severely than his father did, and ten tribes revolt and make Jeroboam their king. These ten tribes become known as the "Northern Kingdom" or the "children of Israel" (see Jer. 32:30). Rehoboam continues to reign in Jerusalem, and his kingdom becomes known as the "Southern Kingdom" or the "house of Judah."

The sad reality is that, after setting up his kingdom, Jeroboam does not encourage the people to worship God. He fears that, if his subjects return to Jerusalem for their annual feasts four times a year, their loyalty will return to the house of David, and they will no longer want him as king. Thus, Jeroboam builds two calves of gold. One he sets up in Bethel, the other he sets up in Dan.

He essentially tells his people, "It is too far for you to go and sacrifice in Jerusalem. See, here are your gods that brought you out of Egypt. Come here and sacrifice to them and worship them." He sets the example by calling a feast day and sacrificing to the golden calves. The people follow Jeroboam's example, and it is awfully sad to note that every king who takes the throne in the Northern Kingdom after this experience is an idol worshiper until they are finally destroyed as a kingdom.

I shake my head in disbelief and find it hard to understand how they could make the same mistake again in worshipping the golden calf. Did they not do this before? and did they not see the results of their actions? Worshipping a golden calf—why would anyone think that such was an acceptable practice when they knew who the God of Israel is and what He had done for them as a people?

The truth is that most people are more than happy to follow the leader without having to think for themselves about their actions and the consequences. When talking to people about why they do things, they will often reply, "Oh, this is how my parents and grandparents did it, so that's why we do it." That, unfortunately, is not a good enough reason to keep doing something. All people should find out for themselves why they are doing what they are doing, especially when it comes to worship, or they might be worshipping the beast and his image without even realizing it.

> *"How will I know what or who the beast and his image is?" I hear you ask.*

"How will I know what or who the beast and his image is?" I hear you ask. That is a great question and one we will have to examine so that you can know without a doubt who the beast is, as well as his image.

I love the fact that Jesus invites us in the words, "Come now, and let us reason together" (Isaiah 1:18). He does not want a form of worship that is impersonal or based on habits. He would like us to talk with Him, ask Him questions, and reason with Him. That will prevent our religion from becoming dead, habitual, and a formality that is practiced over and over without making any real sense or change in our lives.

Chapter 9

The Beast and Its Image

If you type the phrase, "the beast," into a Bible search engine, you will come up with many texts containing those two words. Up until Daniel's use of the term "beast," it has referred to animals used in sacrifice, such as the heifer, or a wild animal of the field. Yet, in Daniel chapter 7, the prophet has a dream about four "beasts," and these "beasts" represent dominions or world powers.

The beasts in Daniel's dream are describing the same world powers that Nebuchadnezzar's dream of the image had described. Do you remember the dream of King Nebuchadnezzar? The story is found in Daniel 2. The king had a dream that he could not remember. He knew that it was so important that he was prepared to kill all his wise men if they could not tell him the dream and its meaning.

Daniel was the only one who was able to tell the king his dream because he was a child of God, and it is only God who can reveal what people think and dream and what it means. The image of King Nebuchadnezzar's dream represented various dominions or world powers that would rule from that time until the close of earth's history when Jesus returns to earth.

Daniel's dream is about four beasts coming up out of the sea. The first one is a lion. The lion represents Babylon. It fascinates me how archaeologists have dug up the ruins of Babylon and found that their brick work was inscribed with the symbol of a lion. The beasts of Daniel's dream correlate to the image in King Nebuchadnezzar's dream, and that is how we have the concept that a beast can represent a dominion or world power in Bible prophecy. Additionally, an angel gives Daniel the interpretation later in chapter 7 and tells him the beasts represent kingdoms (verse 17).

The next beast in Daniel's dream that came up out of the sea was a bear. This bear is higher on one side than on the other. We know from the interpretation that God gave Daniel (and history confirms it) that the second kingdom to rule after Babylon was that of the Medes and the Persians. The Persian part of the empire was greater than that of the Medes, and that is why one side of the bear is higher than the other side. The three ribs in his mouth are a symbol of the three empires that the Persian king conquered.

The third beast is leopard-like with four wings and four heads. The world kingdom that conquered the Medes and Persians was that of Alexander the Great, who was the first king of Greece. The speed with which he conquered the Medo-Persian empire is depicted by his four wings. The four heads are symbolic of his four generals who, after Alexander's untimely death, divided his kingdom because they just could not work together.

The fourth beast in Daniel's dream was dreadful, terrible, and exceedingly strong. It devoured with huge iron teeth and broke its opponents into pieces and trampled the residue with its feet. This beast showed no mercy. The Roman Empire was known for

Chapter 9: The Beast and Its Image

its brutality and reigning as with an iron fist. The Romans were responsible for fine tuning execution by crucifixion, and they meant it to be the cruellest form of torture known to mankind.

This beast also has ten horns. While Daniel is looking at this beast and its horns, a little horn appears on the beast's head and starts to grow. As it grows, it uproots three of the other ten horns. This horn, however, has eyes and a mouth like a man. Daniel tells us in verse 15 that this vision grieved and troubled him, so he approaches one of the messengers standing by, most probably his accompanying angel, who makes clear to Daniel what his vision means.

He does not say much about the first three beasts, except to say that they are kings that rise to power, but he spends quite a few verses explaining the fourth beast and his little horn power. This little horn becomes quite powerful as he is able to uproot three of the ten horns, which represent ten kings that come up out of the fourth beast. This little horn also speaks great words against God, the most High, and the horn wears out the saints of the most High. He thinks to change times and laws, and the saints are given into his hands for a specific period of time (see verse 25). This little horn that grows on the head of the beast is given specific characteristics to help us identify who it is.

If we continue searching through our Bibles after Daniel, we see that the term "beast" reverts back to referring to the animals of the field, just as it was prior to Daniel—that is, until we reach Revelation. In Revelation, "beast" is again used to refer to a kingdom or dominion that rules over people. It is not surprising that Daniel and Revelation use the same kind of imagery. After all, they are intricately linked prophetic books which both predict what is going to happen in the future.

In one of our previous chapters, we took a good look at who the woman riding on the beast was. The parallel can be drawn between the little horn that also rides on the beast, and if you study into it, you will find that the similarities between the woman and the little horn are so close that the only conclusion you can come to is that the little horn and the woman on the beast are the same entity.

I think it is also apparent that the beast is not representing God and His kingdom but representing a kingdom or dominion that opposes God and His law. Go with me to Revelation 13. This chapter talks about two beasts, one coming out of the sea and one coming from the earth. When reading verses 1–10, I wonder if you can pick up similarities between this beast and the little horn. John is standing on the sand, and the first beast he mentions comes out of the sea. The fourth beast mentioned by Daniel also came out of the sea.

> *It is also apparent that the beast is not representing God and His kingdom but representing a kingdom or dominion that opposes God and His law.*

The first beast in Revelation 13 has the mouth of a lion, feet like a bear, and it is shaped like a leopard. Wow! Where have we seen these images before? That's right—in Daniel 7. The difference between the two is that John's beast is a combination of three beasts, with the same number of heads as the four beasts in Daniel combined but with ten crowns. I would like you to notice who gives this beast his power. Look at Revelation 13:2, which says: "And the dragon gave him his power." Wow, so there is an even fiercer power that gives this beast his power.

Hmm, what do we know about the dragon? Just turn back to Revelation 12, verse 9, and you will see that the great dragon is the old serpent, the devil, or Satan. The beast from the sea gets his power from Satan. Let's dig a bit deeper into Revelation 13. It says in verses 3 and 4 that the world wondered after the beast and worshipped it. Hey, our warning in the third angel's message is to not worship the beast and his image, and yet we are told that the world wonders after the beast and worships him.

In Revelation 13, verses 5 through 8, we are given even more characteristics about the beast. He has a mouth and speaks blasphemy against God, His name (or character), and tabernacle. Keep in mind that the tabernacle was what God used to teach the children of Israel about the plan of salvation. This beast is also

Chapter 9: The Beast and Its Image 73

given power to carry on for forty-two months. If each month has 30 days, how many days would that be? Using simple arithmetic, 42 x 30 = 1260 prophetic days.

In Daniel's prophecy, the beast was given power for a time, times, and the dividing of time. A time is equal to one year or 360 days, as they used to calculate it in Bible times. "Times" is two years, i.e., 720 days, and a dividing of time will be half a year, or 180 days. If we add those up, the equation looks like this: 360 + 720 + 180 = 1260 prophetic days. Mmmm, that's the same time period we just saw in Revelation. This time period also happens to coincide with the Dark Ages mentioned in the previous chapter.

Prophetic days, according to Ezekiel 4:6 and Numbers 14:34, can be substituted at the ratio of one day for one year. The conclusion to the matter is that the beast in Revelation 13, with his ten heads and ten crowns, is the same as the little horn in Daniel 7. The beast is at war with God's people. He wants to destroy them.

Papal Rome started rising to power during the Roman Empire's rulership, and history tells us that, in AD 538, Papal Rome defeated the last of its major enemies, thereby becoming the most powerful political force in the then-known world. It used its power not only for political and financial gain but also for religious purposes. Millions of people were persecuted and put to death during its reign. It took away the Bible from the people and claimed to be infallible. "Infallible" means incapable of making mistakes in understanding and interpreting the Bible. Even today we see that it still holds onto the claim that it is incapable of making such mistakes.

Maintaining dominance is the big reason why Papal Rome would persecute anyone who went against its doctrines and beliefs or who dared to challenge its way of thinking and doing. The Bible truth found in the third angel's message is saying that anyone who worships the beast and his image will suffer the punishment of God—not because He enjoys punishing sinners but because He has warned that sin will be destroyed and anyone who chooses to hang onto sin will be destroyed with it.

The third angel's message is warning those who worship the beast and his image about the consequences that will follow as a result. It is clear that the message is using symbolism, just as the other two angels who preceded it did, and we have managed to understand who or what the beast power is.

Worshipping the beast would mean following the beliefs and traditions that the beast upholds. Now that we know who or what the beast is, it is easy to stay away from it, isn't it? But what about his image?

Remember how King Nebuchadnezzar made a golden image to replicate what he had seen in his dream? Yet, there was a big difference—he made the whole image of gold to show God that he, King Nebuchadnezzar, was going to change what God had predicted.

We know that was not successful, but we have a clear picture of what an image could look like. It is a replica of the real thing. Today we see that there are many churches that still embrace the image of the beast. For instance, churches that promote and keep the first day of the week holy are imitating the beast. They are choosing to follow manmade traditions and laws over a clear, Bible-based commandment. The Roman Catholic Church itself is proud to admit that they were the ones who changed the day of worship from the seventh day to the first day.

There are also churches that sprinkle their babies and call it baptism rather than following Jesus' example of being baptized by going under the water. Jesus was not sprinkled as a baby and neither should we. Baptism should happen when you are old enough to understand the meaning and can ask to be baptized, when it is your choice to be baptized, not the choice of your parents or others. This, too, is an imitation of the beast, and you can go back in history and trace the origin of infant baptism to the Roman Catholic Church.

The thought that you can talk to the dead is quickly becoming extremely popular. I had a friend who was willing to pay a large sum of money to someone who claimed to talk to dead people. My friend's mother had died, and my friend wanted to ask her questions about life. I warned her to stay away because these people were deceiving her. The reality is that the Roman Catholic Church has been teaching, for hundreds of years, that we should pray to the dead saints, especially Mary, the mother of Jesus.

The image of the beast does not look much different when you come to think of it. The Bible is truly clear about the condition of people when they die and the reality that they know nothing. You will find that in Ecclesiastes 9:5, 6. Why would you be tempted to think that you can talk with or pray to a dead person?

One of the really scary things is that, when you are worshipping the beast, you will accept the church's teaching that when you die, you will go to a place called purgatory. It is probably best described as a waiting room, but it has elements of torture in it. Dying, therefore, becomes quite scary, for that is when torture will begin, and it will be based on the life you have lived here on earth. The length of time you spend in purgatory will depend on the type of person you have been, but it will also depend on your family's ability to pay large sums of money to the church after you die that will help to shorten your time in purgatory.

The belief is that the time in purgatory is a time of cleansing, and the cleansing involves torture. The reality is that this is so far from Bible truth, it isn't funny. Biblically, we know that everyone who dies goes into a deep sleep and waits for the return of Jesus, either as their friend and Saviour or as their enemy, based on the choices they have made while they were alive and able to make those choices. At Jesus' return, He will reward everyone according to their choices.

The truth of the matter is that there are individuals who do not want to go to heaven. How unfair would it be to take away their choice? I think of Cain, Adam's first son, and how he had no desire to be in God's presence. God did not force him to go against his own will, and, still today, He will not force anyone to do what they don't want to do. He allows us to have freedom of choice.

The Bible is clear about the way in which Jesus will return. He will come in the clouds, and every eye will see it happen. The image of the beast has all kinds of variations of this, including things like being taken away secretly (called the "secret rapture"). Another common belief is that, after you die, you will come back to this world in a different form, maybe as a cat, a mouse, or a cockroach, depending on the life you lived, and you will keep reincarnating until you reach a state of perfection. These are not biblical principles, so please stay away from them, for they are a "worshipping the beast and his image" religion.

I guess it is perfectly safe to say that any religion that places traditions or customs above the Word of God is wondering after the beast and his image. Does that mean that all people practicing those religions are evil? No, there are many faithful Christians in these religions that are still waiting to hear the truth, and when the time is right, God will reveal to them their errors, and they will then make the changes that are needed. Maybe in reading this book you realize that there are beliefs and practices in your own life that you are not sure are entirely correct or in agreement with the Word of God.

Everybody is responsible for his or her own choices and decisions, and everyone will be given the same opportunity to choose between good and evil. The sad truth is that there are elements of image worship in almost every religion or church in the world. We all have a responsibility to keep our church as a pure bride, ready to meet the Groom, Jesus, when He comes to fetch her.

The third angel's message, just like the first and second messages, is preached to everyone living on the earth. It is a warning to those who are worshipping in a false religion, but it also points out another group of people—a people who keep the commandments of God and have the faith of Jesus. There are two groups of people: both will receive the reward they have chosen, either eternal life or eternal death. We all have a choice, and now is the time to make that choice.

Chapter 10

Patience of the Saints

Looking at the culture of today gives me the idea that patience is a good value while grace has been long forgotten and lost. The virtue of patience comes from the days when Nana and Pop were children with lots of time to be patient. Think about your own life. Letter writing is no longer something we do, as it takes too long to receive a response. SMS or email is our preferred way of communicating because the results and replies are instantaneous.

I can see my daughter rolling her eyes at the thought of writing a letter, saying, "No, that takes too long. Snapchat works for me, and the benefit is you don't even need to write about what you are doing; you can just take a picture." I was surprised to see a badly taken photo of an unmade bed and two human legs. The person was sending the message that he was on his bed doing nothing. Another way in which communication has been shortened is text abbreviations, such as *wud* (what you doin'), *k* (okay), and *hbu* (how 'bout you), to name just a few.

"Here is the patience of the saints ..."

We have been conditioned to be impatient when things seem to take too long. We get impatient when things drag on, so we have invented fast food, fast transport, and even faster technology, among other things, and we have evolved into fast-paced humans. We carry this into our religious lives as well, as we want God to give us quick answers to our prayers and to work miracles to solve our problems quickly.

I did a quick search in the Bible on the word *patience*. (Yes, we can do that faster now as well!) The results were surprising. The words "patience" and "affliction," or "tribulation," seemed to go together quite often, reminding us to be patient during bad times, to take comfort in God's Word, and to remember that He is in control.

While pondering the word "patience," I was reminded of the story, in Matthew 25, of the ten virgins. They had a special job of providing light for the wedding ceremony. They all knew what their job and purpose were, so they waited patiently for the bridegroom to come. In their patient state, however, they fell asleep. Falling asleep was not necessarily the problem; it was falling asleep without properly preparing for what they had been asked to do that was the problem.

We know and understand that the oil that the five foolish virgins ran out of was symbolic of the Holy Spirit. Those who woke up without enough oil represent the class of believers who do not allow the Holy Spirit to transform their lives. To be ready when Jesus comes to take us home, we need to be changed, or, as the Bible puts it, we need to be re-created into the image of God.

When we look at the last part of the third angel's message, we see that, during this time, when the world seems to be worshipping the beast and its image, there is a group of people who are patiently enduring the tribulations and difficulties coming their way because they are choosing to keep the commandments of God and the faith of Jesus. "Knowing *this*, that the trying of your faith worketh patience. But let patience have *her* perfect work, that ye may be perfect and entire, wanting nothing" (James 1:3–4).

When we look around us and realize that worshipping the image of the beast has become so prominent and acceptable, it surely tries our faith as we are brought face to face with what we believe and why we believe it. However, let's look at James 1:3 again, but this time putting it in easier-to-understand language: "Know this, that the testing of your belief in God as Creator and Saviour is bringing about endurance in you."

All through the New Testament, reference is made to being patient during trials. Having endurance or patience during a trial is by no means easy. We look at the situation that is causing us grief, and we want to fix it or somehow have it fixed right away. How easy it is to give up or throw in the towel.

I had the privilege of going to a swimming carnival and watching my daughter compete. The whistle blew, and they were off. She was doing so well and keeping up with the swimmer in the lead. However, about a meter before the finish, she looked up to see how far the edge of the pool was, and, in that moment, two other swimmers finished the race before she did. It was so sad to watch it happen as she was so close to getting second place, but she had become impatient and wanted to know where the edge was instead of just patiently continuing with what she was meant to do—swim.

As Christians, we often do the same thing. Instead of patiently enduring through the trials, we stop to look around and ask, "Why me?" We compare ourselves with others, thinking: *Oh, I'm not as good a Christian as they are. There must be something wrong with me. I must just not be Christian material.* We look back at ourselves and our trials, and we get discouraged. We forget that we were meant to patiently endure our trials with our eyes fixed on Jesus. He is our goal! (See Hebrews 12:1.)

Looking to others and comparing our progress can be very discouraging and distracting. It could also go the other way if we look at others and pat ourselves on the back with the thoughts that we are at least not as bad or sinful as they are. Either way, we have taken our eyes off Jesus, our goal, and are looking to self. Never do you see runners who are serious about running looking around to see where they are at in comparison to the other runners. No way! They have studied the route, and their eyes are fixed on the goal. What the other runners are doing is the other runners' business. Each runner, who wants to win, is focused on running his or her race.

> *The whistle blew, and they were off. She was doing so well and keeping up with the swimmer in the lead.*

Let us get back to the third angel and the statement, "Here is the patience of the saints." In other words, in this place and at this time in earth's history, the saints are running the race without being distracted by false doctrines and beliefs. They are going through trials, but they are aware that the trials are all part of their character development. They have studied and continue to study the map, the Word of God, and their eyes are fixed on their goal, who also happens to be their best friend and Saviour, Jesus Christ.

Where are your eyes, young reader? Are you being pulled from side to side by all kinds of strange ideas and beliefs, or are you grounded in a "Thus saith the Lord" relationship with your Saviour? Are you daily going to God's Word and digging for the special treasures He has especially hidden there for you? No one else can find them for you; you are the only one who can find the treasures hidden for you. Likewise, you are not able to find treasures for others; only they can find them for themselves. Oh, you are welcome to share the treasures you have found and enjoy what others have found, but God has purposefully hidden treasure just for you. It is there in the Bible, waiting to be discovered by you.

In the last part of Revelation 14:12, we note, by the word "keep," that these saints are keeping safe or guarding something. There seems to be something worth protecting to ensure that it does not get lost or damaged. We will investigate that in our next chapter.

Chapter 11

What Is It Worth to You?

In the very beginning of this world's history, God planted a garden. It was an incredibly special garden. It was more beautiful than you or I could even imagine and had everything you and I could ever need or want and then some. It was known as the garden of Eden. The word "garden" means "enclosure," and the word "Eden" means "pleasure or delight." Therefore, this garden was known as an enclosure of pleasure or delight.

In this garden were two special trees. The one tree was referred to as "the tree of life," and, if Adam and Eve continued to eat of its fruit, they would be immortal, meaning they would never die. The other tree was known as "the tree of knowledge of good and evil." Eating it would have other consequences.

Adam and Eve were placed in the garden, and it was to be their home. They were asked to care for the garden and look after the animals; they were instructed to enjoy all that was prepared for them; and free range was given them to eat of every tree in the garden except for one. In the entire garden, there was only one tree from which they were asked to stay away. That tree was in the middle of the garden, and it wasn't much different from any of the other hundreds of trees in the garden. However, Adam and Eve were asked and reminded again and again to please not eat from it.

It really was not such a big, hard thing they were asked to do. There were many, many other trees in the garden from which they could choose. This one singular tree was there as a test of loyalty. All went well for a while until, one day, Eve found herself alone and not by Adam's side. She had wandered off, and, before she knew it, she was standing by the tree in the middle of the garden—the same tree they had been warned about.

Instead of turning on her heels and leaving the place, she dawdled and looked, and then heard a very melodious and inviting voice speaking to her from within the tree. Eve was mesmerized; she was spell bound. We know the end of the story. She ate of the fruit of the tree and then gave some of it to Adam, and he ate of it too. How sad! They were not eating because they were hungry for food; they ate because they had been convinced that they were missing out on something.

For their safety and the safety of the entire human race, they were asked to leave their garden home. Their choices led them to lose their beautiful home, their enclosure of pleasure. "But why?" you may ask. The reason was that the tree of life was in the garden, and it gave immortality to whoever ate of its fruit. Because Adam and Eve had sinned, God did not want sin to be immortalized, and that is why He needed to stop them from eating of that tree.

God was fair.

To keep them away from the tree of life, an angel with a flaming sword was placed at the entrance of the garden. Some people might say that God was not kind to send them out of the garden,

Chapter 11: What Is It Worth to You?

but, to be honest, God was fair, and fairness does not always seem kind at the time. He knew that, if they, as sinners, continued to eat of the fruit of the tree of life, they would live forever with the consequences of sin.

I have only been alive for just over 40 years, but I can tell you that I am already tired of the effects that sin has had on me and those I love, not to mention the things I hear about in the news. I would be awfully miserable if I had to continue like this forever and ever. Imagine cancer patients having to live forever with their cancer and its effects, or imagine people who are paralysed and in a wheelchair because of a car crash caused by a drunk driver having to live forever in their condition. That would be torture. I believe that as God, in His wisdom, looked down the course of time, He mercifully put an angel to guard the tree.

Generally, you would only guard things that are important or valuable to you. Immortal life is valuable to God, and He intended life to be enjoyed. People are not going to guard some few river pebbles that they pick up while going on a nature walk. However, if they discover that a river pebble they have found is a gemstone or gold, they would altogether change the way they looked at it and cared for it. They would keep it safe and secure. When something has value, we keep it safe or guard it.

> *He knew that, if they, as sinners, continued to eat of the fruit of the tree of life, they would live forever with the consequences of sin.*

The scripture says: "Here is the patience of the saints: here *are* they that keep the commandments of God" (Revelation 14:12). The saints are guarding God's commandments and keeping them safe. Safe from what, you might ask? Safe from misuse or contamination maybe? God says in His commandments not to have any other gods besides Him, not to bow down and worship idols, and not to use His name out of sacred context. These all seem simple, but the group of people, spoken of in Revelation—the ones not worshipping the beast and his image—are guarding these commandments. They are keeping them safe from contamination and pollution. Let us look at them individually to see what that could look like. You will find them in Exodus 20.

The first commandment says: Don't have any other gods before Jehovah God. Have you ever loved something so much that you just could not think to live without it? You often spoke about it to others and thought about it, even at times when you should have been thinking about something else. It occupied your every thought. The truth is that God says He wants to be that single most important thought to us. We should so value and love Him that we often talk and regularly think of and about Him.

We should guard our thoughts to ensure that nothing takes the place that Jesus should be occupying, letting nothing keep us from spending time with Him in His Word and prayer or looking forward to our time together. Having no other gods before God means that nothing is more important to us than Jesus and having a relationship with Him.

The second commandment says: Don't bow down to any image or the likeness of anything. Having an idol can be very subtle. I work four days a week and simply love my job. However, not too long ago, I realized that my job was taking over my life. It wasn't hard for that to happen since I enjoy what I do for a living, but I was sacrificing my family time to work, and I even began to rush my private worship time so I could get back to—you guessed it—work. I was most certainly bowing down to an idol, and I needed to confess and ask God to forgive me and set me free from its control. Now I decidedly guard that commandment when it comes to my work and only give it the time it requires, not the time my family and God deserve.

The third commandment says: Don't take the name of the Lord in vain. Have you ever had friends over, and, before you knew it, your siblings and you were in an argument about something really silly and small? The friend just stands and watches while you and your siblings are heatedly disputing over the facts. When all eventually dies down and there is a moment to rationally think about what just happened, you realize that you have just taken the name of the Lord in vain.

Chapter 11: What Is It Worth to You?   85

No, no, I'm not saying that, during the argument, you used God's name to hurl insults at your sibling. I mean that your actions contradicted what a Christian life should look like. Instead of showing kindness, patience, and love, you displayed selfish interest and self-love. To not take God's name in vain is so much more than just avoiding using His name to curse. It is making sure that, when others look at us and our behaviour, they can see Jesus.

Each of the Ten Commandments is packed with so much more meaning than just the words we read. However, it is the fourth commandment, as we have seen in previous chapters, that is particularly interesting. The dragon does not want this commandment honoured or kept. The fourth commandment is extremely specific in its requirements, and, when we read it, it appears to be in the format of an invitation.

Have you ever received an invitation to a party? If it doesn't have specific elements, it isn't a real invitation. For instance, imagine receiving an invitation that doesn't say from whom it came. What if the invitation just gives a hint about who it came from, but, as you continue reading, it gives no date or time for the event, nor does it mention anything about where it is going to be held. If that were the case, it would not be a true invitation. It might have the words, "You are invited," written on it, but the truth is that, without the essential elements I have mentioned, it just isn't an invitation, and it would be rather disappointing to receive something like that.

The fourth commandment, however, has all the essential elements to make it a true invitation. You can find it in Exodus 20:8–11. It begins with the word "Remember." It is a special event, and the Inviter does not want you to forget that you have been invited. A bride-to-be will often send a "Save the date" refrigerator magnet to ensure that her guests have their calendars clear for her big day. It is kind of like the "Remember" in the fourth commandment.

Date and time: "The seventh day is the Sabbath." Can there be any confusion regarding when this event will take place? Sadly, yes, many people have tried to change calendars to start on Monday so that they finish off on Sunday, but it's not hard to realize from history that the seventh day has been and will always be Saturday.

Inviter: "The LORD thy God who created heaven and earth." It is rather clear who sent the invitation, and you do not need to guess to know who sent it. The invitation gives the name and title of the One who sent it.

The Sabbath invitation goes on to give additional information about the event, such as the theme and what the attendee can expect. This is not uncommon for an invitation. When hosting a party or event, you will want the people to know what kind of event to which they are invited. Is it a birthday party or wedding? and will there be a theme? For instance, if you are having the party at a pool or the beach, your guests need to know to bring appropriate clothing. You have expectations of your guests, and, through the invitation, they will know what is expected of them.

In the fourth commandment invitation, we are asked to keep it holy and not do any work or make anyone else work for us either. How exciting it is to receive an invitation for every week of the year, every year! Did you realize how popular you are? You have a weekly standing invitation from the Creator of the world!

Thus far, we have looked at the first four of the Ten Commandments, and we are told that the group of people not worshipping or following after the beast are guarding the commandments of God. It is clear that this group of people will have a very special regard for these four commandments and will keep the seventh day, which, in English, we call "Saturday," as God's holy day. This makes them stand out above the crowd. While most professing Christians worship on the first day of the week, Sunday, there is a small number of Christians throughout the world who honour the seventh day, Saturday. The next six commandments will be important to them as well, and they will guard and look after them too.

The fifth commandment says: Honour your father and mother. Unfortunately, there is not much of this happening in our world today. My daughter was encouraged by friends to do something that went against my wishes, and she was convinced that my views were old-fashioned and my counsel did not deserve attention. Unfortunately, these friends are not the minority group.

The sixth commandment says: Don't kill. This commandment not only refers to the literal sense of not killing, but also to the figurative sense, such as not hating someone in your heart. It's easy to kill someone's feelings and character through our actions.

The seventh commandment says: Don't commit adultery. This world has become so diseased that broken families are the norm, and children especially suffer when this commandment is not being kept, honoured, and guarded.

The eighth commandment says: Don't take what does not belong to you. How sad that some people think that they can help themselves to what they have not worked for or earned. It is even sadder when people are prepared to take what belongs to others—including things such as their characters—and that robbery goes hand-in-hand with the next commandment.

The ninth commandment says: Don't bear false witness. So many people enjoy good gossip. Yet, gossip is very damaging. I wonder if many realize that, through gossip, Lucifer carried out his plan of deception in heaven. He went from one angel to another, spreading, in the form of gossip, lies and rumours about God and His character. He robbed God of His character by telling lies, and, before they all knew what was happening, there was much confusion, and war broke out. Spreading rumours about people not only steals their self-worth and dignity, but it often requires lies to be added to the rumour to give it sensation.

The tenth commandment says: Don't covet what others have. This commandment surely is an interesting one. I have three children, and, on a regular basis, they will tell me about a friend who has this new toy or that new gadget, and they will express the wish that they could have one too. Not being happy because of what another person has that is special is covetousness, and we are warned against it. Often, if we do not guard against such desires, it will lead to breaking many of the other commandments to be able to secure possession of the coveted item. Satan was covetous of the worship and honour that Christ, the Son of God, was receiving, and he resorted to breaking each one of the commandments to secure the adoration for himself.

It is only through the power and grace of God that we can be the saints of Revelation 14 who keep God's commandments.

Chapter 12

And Keep the Faith of Jesus

It is said that your faith is not tested in times of ease and peace, but in times of trial and hardship. I went through a particularly hard time in my life, and it brought me face-to-face with what I believed about God as my Father and His love for me. It surely was not a nice or comfortable experience, but, looking back now, the experience was valuable to me in that I am now more firmly grounded in my faith and I have grown closer to Jesus my Saviour than ever before. Thus, I can testify that the testing of my faith worked endurance (see James 1:3).

The definition of *faith* is "a conviction or belief with respect to man's relationship to God and divine things." The Bible tells us, "Now faith is the substance," or foundation, "of things hoped for, the evidence," or proof, "of things not seen" (Hebrews 11:1). I am going to give you a practical example of faith, and hopefully that will make it a little clearer.

Every day, I sit down at my dining table to have at least one meal. When all is on the table, I take a seat. I don't think about it much; I just pull the chair closer and sit on it. I have faith that the chair will hold my weight, so I sit down. The foundation of my faith is in the chair holding my weight; the proof is me sitting on it.

However, when I decide to stand on the chair so that I can reach something at the top of my cupboard, my faith is tested regarding the chair, as I no longer know whether it will be strong enough to bear my weight. My faith in the chair's ability to do what I need it to do—to keep me from hurting myself and help me reach the top of the cupboard—exercises my faith.

> *When I decide to stand on the chair so that I can reach something at the top of my cupboard, my faith is tested regarding the chair.*

In spiritual matters, it is very much the same. My foundation of faith is that God is able to save me from this world that is filled with sin and from my own life of sin, and the proof of my faith is when I daily take His hand and walk with Him.

"Here *are* they that keep the commandments of God, and the faith of Jesus" (Revelation 14:12). We looked at "keep the commandments of God" in the previous chapter. Now we will look at keeping "the faith of Jesus." To understand the phrase, "the faith of Jesus," we need to look at Jesus' life and what His faith was like while He was here on earth.

Jesus had many trials. Life here on this earth was by no means easy for Him. One time in particular was when He was in the wilderness after He had been baptized. His enemy, the devil, was determined to destroy Him. He waited until Jesus was physically weak and hungry before he brought his three temptations to Jesus. We could say that Jesus' faith was being tested. However, Jesus resisted each temptation with the words "It is written" and a promise from God's Word.

Chapter 12: And Keep the Faith of Jesus

Jesus did not rely on His own strength to resist; He referred to His Father's word. Jesus was definitely hungry after not eating for forty days, and turning stones into loaves of bread could have seemed very inviting, but His foundation was in His Father's word and in His Father's ability to sustain Him. Never ever did Jesus use His power for His own good. His faith was that His Father would take care of all His needs and provide for Him.

Looking at the closing scenes of Jesus' life and ministry in the garden of Gethsemane, at the judgement hall, and on the cross gives us a clear picture of His faith in His Father. In the garden, Jesus has asked His three closest disciples to come with Him. They have never seen Jesus like this before. He is physically weighed down with a burden that seems too heavy for Him to bear. He is clearly struggling with something, but they do not know what it is.

They have been asked to wait at a certain spot and pray while Jesus goes a little farther to pray by Himself. Unfortunately, they neglect the prayer part, and, in no time, they are all fast asleep. Jesus is in a huge struggle. He fears that the separation from His Father will be permanent, and He fears the torture and pain that He knows He is about to endure. He longs for someone to give Him comfort, but every time He goes to find His friends, He finds them fast asleep.

Jesus has a decision. He must choose whether to leave this world and allow His sleeping friends—and the whole human race, for that matter—to work out their own future. Yet, He sees the history and the future of the human race and the reality that, without His sacrifice, all humans will forever be lost. Such a view overrules His fears for His own welfare. He puts His faith in His Father's will, believing that He will bring Him through this trial. Jesus decides for humankind without any regard for what it will cost Him.

None of us will ever be required to endure the severity of the trial Jesus endured, and He endured it for us. But we must still choose whether we will accept His substitution. There are people who choose not to accept the sacrifice that Jesus made for them, and they will have to endure the consequences of their choice. Such does not have to be your story or mine, nor does it have to be anyone's story, for Jesus' sacrifice was sufficient for every human who was ever born and who will ever be born.

I just love the way that Jesus recently taught me this concept of faith in a very practical way. There has been a lot of stress and worry in my life, and, unfortunately, my parents were the ones on whom I had subconsciously chosen to take out my frustrations. They, in a very loving way, pointed out what I had been doing and how mean I had been. The Holy Spirit very gently confirmed it.

I felt awful. They were right; I had been mean and angry in how I treated them. I asked for their forgiveness and then went to our heavenly Father and asked Him for His forgiveness too. I had clearly been breaking the fifth commandment. James, through inspiration, clearly stated that, if we break one commandment, we break them all. I was guilty. I deserved the wages of sin, for I had earned it by my actions.

The accuser, the devil, was very ready to remind me of what a rotten, awful daughter I am, and he loves to bring up the past and then point to the future to paint a very discouraging picture. However, my faith jumped into action. I was reminded of Ezekiel 36:25, 26, in which God promises to wash me clean from all my filthiness and then give me a new heart and spirit. He promises to take away the heart of stone and give me a heart of flesh.

I had a choice: I could either believe the lies that Satan was telling about me and how hopeless my situation was, or I could look to Jesus, who has paid the price for my sin, and accept God's promise of a new heart and life. I chose to have faith in God. He is faithful and has not failed anyone. My choice to believe in Him is safe. In this, my faith was exercised.

The first morning after all this had taken place, I woke up feeling very unsure, almost like a baby taking her first steps. Such steps are very unsteady, and they take a lot of concentration and effort. I felt like that—very unsafe and unsure about whether it was even possible for me to change—but I dumped all my fears at Jesus' feet and asked Him to please help me that day.

Guess what? He did! I was able to show my parents the tender, loving care they deserve. I know that in my own strength, I am fully capable of being mean and unkind, but, with Jesus in control, I am being the kind of daughter that He wants me to be—kind, loving, and helpful. The bonus is that I'm also happy again. Yes, my stress is still there, but I now choose to deal with it differently instead of making it someone else's problem. That is faith in action. Faith, however, does not sit around doing nothing. Oh no! It puts works into action. It changes bad habits into good ones, bad actions into good actions, and bad thoughts into trusting, believing thoughts. Faith is the victory over sin that we all so desperately need.

Keeping, or guarding, the faith of Jesus means becoming more like Him each and every day. It includes admitting that we need to be changed and that our sin needs to be washed away, then it includes asking Jesus to give us the faith to go and sin no more.

It is very sad to see how many people believe that, because we are born into a sinful world, we are doomed to be sinners until we die. The truth is that Jesus was born into a sinful world, but He lived a holy and perfect life, and, in Matthew 5:48, He taught that we need to be perfect as our Father in heaven is perfect. Do you think Jesus would be asking of us something He knows is totally impossible for us to do?

The reality is that, even as people back in Jesus' day, many people today do not quite understand the truth behind what He is saying. If we look at the Pharisees of Jesus' time, we see that they thought they were earning their perfection by keeping laws—especially all their extra made-up laws. On the outside, people looked at them and thought they were perfect. They never seemed to do anything that violated the law.

However, inside, their hearts were filled with pride. As an illustration, I can bake the best cake and decorate it so that it looks professional, but if I forget to put in the sugar, no one is going to want to eat it after the first bite. It might look like a cake and smell like a cake, but when anyone tastes it, they will know very obviously that it is not a cake, but a fake!

Jesus really does not want an outward show of perfection; He wants our hearts. He wants to take out our stony, pride-filled hearts and give us a heart of flesh (see Ezekiel 36:26). In other words, He wants to change the way we think and feel about things.

The faithful group of people spoken of in Revelation 14:12 who do not receive the mark of the beast but receive the seal of God and are enabled to stand when the whole world is wondering after the beast are keeping the commandments of God and the faith of Jesus. These two go together and cannot be separated. You cannot keep God's commandments unless you have the faith of Jesus. Likewise, you will not have the faith of Jesus and knowingly break God's law.

> *I can bake the best cake and decorate it so that it looks professional, but if I forget to put in the sugar, no one is going to want to eat it after the first bite.*

The only way to keep the law of God is by relying on Jesus and His power to transform our sinful characters into the likeness of His perfect and pure character. If we at any time get to the point that we think we can keep the law of God by ourselves, we are without the faith of Jesus because we are relying on our own human abilities.

Normally, having the faith of Jesus will point out my need to be more like Him and move me away from my sinful, lawbreaking ways. Therefore, it is impossible to have one without the other. It is almost the same as saying I choose to have a heartbeat, but I no longer want to breathe. The two functions are quite different and do quite different things to keep my body alive, but I cannot have one without the other and still remain alive. My heart needs to beat, and my lungs need to breathe for my body to be able to do anything related to living.

I need to keep God's law to retain eternal life, but I can only keep it by the faith of Jesus that enabled me to initially obtain eternal life, and that is the beautiful story of salvation. It is not what I have to do for myself but what Jesus can do in me that makes the difference. Is it hard? You can be sure it is no walk in the park. "But why would it be hard?" you may ask. It is because it means engaging in a struggle against self. We are told, "The warfare against self is the greatest battle that was ever fought" (*Steps to Christ*, p. 43). Yet, we are not left to fight it on our own.

Chapter 12: And Keep the Faith of Jesus

Jesus is there, ready to provide us with everything we could possibly require. We just need to call on Him.

Are you ready to be a saint who keeps the commandments of God and has the faith of Jesus?

Here is a prayer for you:

> Dear heavenly Father, thank You for the three angels' messages—messages of warning to help me be ready when Jesus comes. Thank You for being actively involved in my salvation—the process of saving and purifying me for my heavenly citizenship. Father, today I would like to ask for the faith of Jesus that will enable me to keep Your commandments, because without it, I am not able to keep them.
>
> I am sorry for trying to do it all on my own in the past, but thank You for Your forgiveness and righteousness which You use to cover me. Today, I would like to walk by Your side with my hand in Your hand so that I can be one who keeps the commandments of God and has the faith of Jesus.
>
> In the precious and loving name of Jesus I pray, Amen.

TEACH Services, Inc.
PUBLISHING

We invite you to view the complete
selection of titles we publish at:
www.TEACHServices.com

We encourage you to write us
with your thoughts about this,
or any other book we publish at:
info@TEACHServices.com

TEACH Services' titles may be purchased in
bulk quantities for educational, fund-raising,
business, or promotional use.
bulksales@TEACHServices.com

Finally, if you are interested in seeing
your own book in print, please contact us at:
publishing@TEACHServices.com
We are happy to review your manuscript at no charge.